Art for One World

A book for Inspiration – the Magical, Mystical Journeys of three Adventurers. These Journeys will inspire you too. See ideas for Travel art, Eco-Art, Mandalas & a Milestone Book of your life.

You can make a difference!

Art for One World
Inspirational Journey of Della Burford, Dale Bertrand & Kazuko Asaba

conceived and written
by Della Burford©2018
www.dellaburford.com
youtube channel is dellabirdhelmet

Art Activity Cards
written by Della & Dale
created by Dale Bertrand
also in the editing of the book

Photography by Dale Bertrand
Bali workshop Fabrizio Belardetti
Some photos Japan - Kazuko & Ruu's Friends
Sending photos from Japan -Takeshi Ijima & Dan Asaba
Performance 2013 is taken by Masaneo Showjit Sugyama

Copy Editing Laurien Towers
2 liners Jacquie Howardson
Final copy edit Jacquie Howardson
Japanese translation Nick Muhrin
Life outline - Kazuko & Ruu*Ruu in Mexico
Divine section includes Ruu Ruu
& 100% Parade in Japan

ISBN 978-1-927825-07-5
Azatlan Publishing
www.azatlan.com

Dedication

This book is dedicated
to the children of the world
& dream adventurers.
We would also like to dedicate this to three people
in Spirit World – Tedrian Chizik in New York,
(former Producer Director of Dodoland),
to Kazyuji Mitani who performed the Sun Ray
in "Majical Rainbow" in Japan and to little
Adaea Smart, who now is an Angel Princess,
who with the story written for her (Be Well
Princess), helps find our Inner Prince/Princesses.
May their Spirits live on!

Introduction for Book "Art for One World"

Take three biographies the best selling, award-winning author, painter Della Burford , a keeper of special Ancient records , Dale Bertrand, and a successful festival and art School creator - Kazuko Asaba, put them together and share their life stories and you have the book Ärt for One."

The picture book style biography can act as a **catalyst and inspiration** for you to record and chronicle, whether your younger or older, your life. It can also encourage you to ask - "**what** your dreams for the future"? In the book it suggests you make a record of **Milestones** that record the **what, who , how, why, where** & **when** of your life. **Who** is your tribe? **Who** inspired you? Della had a doctor, Dr. Dick Mazurek, who believed in her Art andStory "Journey to Dodoland'" and made it into a full-color picture book. In Dodoland we were able to share the creativity of a land where you could live your dream. This was shared with over 100,00 children via theater in New York and one million on the dodoland.com website.

When synchronicity happens it makes it possible to cross paths with the right people and the right time? Synchronicity came into play when Kazuko "met" Della's book Magical Earth Secrets at a Eco-Fair in Los Angles. Kazuko found it inspiring and used it in her art school for many years and made a children's play of the book in 1998. In 2011 it became a theater production.

Another question answered in the Milestone book is - "**How** have you had transformation in your life"? There are time in our lives that problems become solutions. Dale though a policeman in his early twenties, had a traumatic experience, and later changed his career to the arts and later helped run the Harbourfront Antique Market. In 1977, a hearing loss jump started a "Merlin"journey and he received a gift of ancestral knowledge that resulted in visiting Power Spots in the world and creating 6 books.

A healing miracle happened to Della. The realization that "**all is one**"came to her first in India in 1973, when in her twenties and twice when she was faced with a cancer diagnosis. These setbacks brought her to ask **why** see a bigger picture of her life. Della made an intention to create opportunities to make peace, harmony, creativity and beauty in the world as part of her life. Again thru adversity Della found a deep inner world that she could travel to. She recorded her dreams on Dreams Wheels and now has 40 years to draw on for stories and art. Dreams can guide and heal and she has included messages from her dreams on the most pages of this book as her dreams were like a oracles guiding her to self heal & advising her on keeping the magic in others lives -many of her dream messages were and are for the world.

Kazuko had a setback in 1985 when a student took his life because life seemed hollow and senseless. This caused a transformation and the book tells **how** it influenced her to make the intention and devote her life to helping all children to find a more spiritual, peaceful way and find the bud of creativity and happiness in their lives. She has shared her passion with children all over the world , and at her Art School, Asaba Art Centre and at the Kanazawabunko Festival which was started in a small way from a home space and now has had 20,000 people attend in one day.

So we record the ups and downs on the **Transformational Map** of our lives. In 2011, after the Big Earthquake, many people in Japan desired a transformation. Kazuko told the "Magical Earth Secrets" and the costume designer Ruu* Ruu was in the audience, this is **when** she knew she wanted to love and protect the earth, and produced it into a play. This is featured in the Divine section of the book. Ruu*Ruu was the perfect one as she was shown in a dream she was to design hats to show the angelic, heroic side of humans. They have successfully taken it to thousands in Japan in the production - "Majical Rainbow". It has been at Earth Day Parades & the Kanzawabunko Festival for seven years. .

Della, Dale and Kazuko asked themselves "**When** were we creative"? They discovered many similarities in their lives. They all shared stories, created art, masks, costumes, They all used "making mandala to help others to make sense of their lives". Della's were "**Dream Wheels**" and **Ïnner Dream Mandalas**"'. Dale facilitated "**Four Winds & Four Directions**" Medicine Wheels with hundreds of children in Toronto and with adults in Bali. Kazuko made **Time Mandalas"** which showed ancient time, from the time we were born till now, and future time. She facilitated this in Japan, Laos, Bhutan and at a Sundance.

They asked themselves, "**Where** have we traveled? Dale and Della at an early stage visited Japan and Kazuko visited North America . They all traveled to Europe and India . They all were attracted to the spirituality of the indigenous people. Della and Dale lead programs at the Wandering Spirit Survival School and Kazuko was teaching in New Mexico. They also loved Ancient Cultures . Kazuko found her Spirit Home was Egypt and went 18 times. Dale and Della traveled on Dale's "Merlin Quest" project visiting many Ancient Sites & Power Spots in the world. **Where** have you traveled on your life journey?

Della says, "**We are all one**. We have all have stories of adversity, and learn as they play out . If you look at you lives and **answer basic questions** you will discover the **uniqueness of your journey**. When you ask **why** you may discover a healing in your life? **When** we have synchronicity happen it feels magical. You can make a difference in our world. You can make a book on your **Milestone Journey**. We have so many to thank, and we send our love to them and you. Yes, we are One, and we can all do "**Art for One World**.

Index for Art for One World

	Dale and Della Beginning Cycle 1968 -73-74	page	10
1968	Della and Dale Toronto	page	11
1971	Travelling Europe	page	12
1972	Della and Dale in Europe – Bird Helmet	page	13
1973	Della teaching Design at Humber College	page	14
1973	Health kickstarts Trip to India & "All is one"	page	15,
1973	Della and Dale travel to India	page	16
1974	Della & Dale Second Trip to India	page	17
1973	Friends become part of Dodoland	page	18
1968	**Beginning Cycle Kazuko starts her art school**	page	19
1970	Japanese students make 100 masks/costumes	page	20
1973	Kazuko travels to San Francisco 1970 & Europe in 1973	page	21
1979	**Transformation Cycle 1975-81 1979 India**	page	22
1981	Trip to San Francisco again - Ruth Asawa	page	23
	Della and Dale Transformation Cycle 1975-81	page	24
1976	Dodoland Our Own Studio - Mirvish Village Toronto	page	25
1976	Creation of Dream Wheels	page	26
1977	Della and Dale visit Japan	page	27
1977	Visiting Kyoto & Osaka for Bunraku	page	28
1977	"Journey to Dodoland" published	page	29
1977	Celebation at Acton	page	30
1977	Mum and Dad make Bird Helmet	page	31
1977	Giant Flower Island – Dale's photography	page	32
1979	Symposium for Humanity - Los Angelas	page	33
1979	Rainbow Rose Festival-Los Angles - Mystical Vision	page	34
1979	Project at Wandering Spirit Survival School - Toronto	page	35
1980	Kootenay Annual Fair/Amanda's Birthday	page	36
1980	Dodoland Performance at Easalen	page	37
1980	Dodoland -Museums, Hospitals, Schools N.Y.C.	page	38
1980	Mystical Painting of Symbols	page	39
	Kazuko Medicine Ways 1982 – 1988	page	40
1982	California -San Francisco & Los Angles	page	41
1983	Asaba Art Show at School	page	42
1983	Goddess Nuit in Egypt	page	43
1984	Exhibition in Luxor -18 trips to Egypt	page	44
1985	Social Problem	page	45
1988	20th Anniversary of Art School /Magical Studio Book	page	46
	Dale and Della's Medicine Ways 1982-1988	page	47
1982	Inner City Angel T.O./Project Opportunidad - N.Y.C.	page	48
	Dale's Trip to Wales	page	49
1982	Magic in Me – Dodoland – Gautemala City	page	50
1982	American Indian Community Cente - N.Y.C.	page	51
1982	Vision Quest - Kootenay Valley	page	52
1982	Ceremony for Peace	page	53

1982	Dodoland at St. Peter's Cathedral- Citycorp-N.Y.C.	page 54
1983	Dale Communications Mgr - Harborfront Antique T.O.	page 55
1983	Dodoland at the Smithsonian at Washington D.C.	page 56
1983	Dodoland at Ontario's Hearing Impaired Schools	page 57
1983	Dodoland -Teaching Dreams - Christies St. School -T.O.	page 58
1983	Della at Sunnyview School	page 59
1984	Dale's Trip to Peru	page 60
1984	Roerich Paintings to Prisoners	page 61
1984	Brooklyn Academy of Music	page 62
1985	Magical Earth Secrets Performed in New York	page 63
1985	Angel Sculptures by Pat Brennan	page 64
1985	Black Book & Honoring Synchronicity	page 65
1985	Dale & Della's Wedding	page 66
1985	Painting in the Kootaneys	page 67
1985	Created Dream Hat for Desiree (mother)	page 68
1986	Travels in Wales - Dale, Bill & Patricia Meilan	page 69
1986	Studied Baby Clown with Richard Pochinko	page 70
1987	I.C.A., Ontario Arts Council & Canada Council	page 71
1987	Cape Cod Writer's Conference	page 72
1987	Dedication – Gift of the Rainbow	page 73
1988	Globetree Sweden	page 74
1989	*Wonder Cycle Kazuko 1989-1995*	page 75
1989	Cultural Exchange with Egypt	page 76
1989	Japanese Egyptian Cultural Exchange	page 77
1989	Japanese Children visit Turkey	page 78
1991	Kazuko discovers Della 's Book Magical Earth Secrets	page 79
1992	Kimono/Kachina making - Taos Pueblo	page 80
1992	Pueblo Children's Batik & Corn Dance at Santa Culara	page 81
1993	Japanese Children Visit Northern Pueblo	page 82
1993	Japanese Children Visit Pueblo	page 83
1994	Japanese Children Visit Pueblo	page 84
	Intuition Cycle - Kazuko 1996- 2002	page 85
1997	Iroquois Peace Prayer	page 86
1998	Kazuko creates play from Della Burford's book MES	page 87
1998	Kazuko class visits the Japanese Ainu Tribe -Hokkaido	page 88
1998	First Kanazawabunko Festival	page 89
1989	*Dale and Della's Wonder Cycle 1989-1995*	page 90
1989	Storytelling with David Lertzman Toronto	page 91
1990	Magical Earth Secrets -Canada Wilderness Committee	page 92
1991	Maria Formolo Dance performs Magical Earth	page 93
1992	Friends of the Environment, Writer in Residence	page 94
1993	Magical Earth Secrets as a School Performances	page 95
1995	Dale travels to Chitza Itza – Tulum	page 96
1995	Dodoland Online	page 97

Dale & Della's Third Eye Cycle 1996 - 2002 — page 98

1997	Start up of Children's School in Gaudalajara	page 99
1997	Trip to Wales while teaching in England	page 100
1997	Della teaches in England - Dale multi-media	page 101
2000	Visit Stonehenge	page 102
2000	August Full Moon - Third Eye Painting	page 103
2001	Dale & Della represent Canada at Festival in Korea	page 104
2001	The Angels Come	page 105
2001	The Angels keep Coming	page 106
2001	Peace Scroll created	page 107
2001	Dale teaches E.S.L...Speech Presentation	page 108
2002	Travel Mural - Sounding the Stones - Penn Kemp	page 109

Miracle Cycle Kazuko 2002 - 2009 — page 110

2007	Hazuma music	page 111
2009	Harmony Medicine Wheels - Ghana	page 112
2009	African Story - Coconut Elixir	page 113
2010	Asaba Art Square	page 114
2010	Asaba Art Square	page 115
2010	Asaba Art Square	page 116

Della and Dale's Miracle Cycle 2002-2009 — page 117

2002	Tomhu Huron Roberts - Early Canadian Artist	page 118
2003	South Coast Plaza - Storytelling-Festival of Children	page 119
2004	Mermaid, Synchronicity	page 120
2004	Sacred Places -Visiting Power Spots	page 121
2004	Create your own Healing Story - Holland	page 122
2005	Miracle Galaxy Dream	page 123
2005	Create your own Myth Class - Vancouver	page 124
2005	Sharing Vision - Druidical Quest- Illuminated Books	page 125
2008	Storytelling Mexico - Los Ayala- Gaudalajara	page 126
2008	Visiting Foco Tonal with Dance teacher Gloria	page 127
2008	Eco Project in Korea	page 128
2008	Dale in Haida Gwaii	page 129

Divine Cycle Dale and Della 2010-18 — page 130

2011	Painted Spirit Stories - Book by Aaron Zerah	page 131
2011	Dream of Dream Goddess	page 132
2011	Make an Angel for Japan . Workshop in Toronto	page 133
2011	Improv of Dodoland with Paripurna Dance School	page 134
2012	Studied Painting in Vienna - Visited Klagenfurt	page 135
2012	Storytelling Austria - Arthoff Gallery	page 136
2012	Workshop Spirit of Writing & Art - Balipurna	page 137
2012	We Come Together to Dream	page 138

*Divine Cycle Dale & Della - Kazuko & Ruu*Ruu 2011-2018 page 139*
*2012 Ruu*Ruu Atelier - Tokyo page 140*
2013 Kanazawabunko Festival - Majical Rainbow page 141
2013 Kanazawabunko Festival - Majical Rainbow page 142
2013 Magical Earth Secrets - "Majical Rainbow" Tokyo page 143 - 144
2013 Newtown Peace Park page 145
2013 Journey to a Lotus - "All is one" page 146
2014 Show Della & Wayan Karja 'Dream Wheels' - Bali page 147
2014 Spirit of Writing and Art - 'Bali feeds our Souls' page 148
2014 100% Parade Earth Day Tokyo page 149
2014 Art Show - Imagination Ottawa/Montreal page 150
2014 Dream Class with Robert Moss page 151
2015 Paul Hogan - T.O/Sri Lanka/Cambodia page 152
2015 Della/Dale/Kazuko/RuuRuu meet in Mexico page 153
2015 Storytelling/Dance in Bali page 154 - 156
2015 Nanaimo Art Gallery Residency page 157
2016 Collaboration I Made/Karja & Della – Dream Keys page 158
2016 Visionary Alchemy Show in New York City page 159
2016 Majical Rainbow Tokyo/ page 160
2016 Earth Day Parade honoring Kiyahiro Owanu -Tokyo page 161
2016 Kazuko - Palestine Project page 162
2016 Kazuko Mandalas Laos page 163
2016 Kazuko Mandalas Bhutan page 164
2017 Spirit of Writing & Art /Show Vivesa page 165
2016 Acu- Yoga - Dream Yoga 2018 page 166 - 167
2017 Imagination Reigns page 168
2017 Performance of 'Majical Rainbow' Show page 169
2017 Kazuko - Minnesota Sundance Mandala page 170
2017 Kazuko - Memorial for Dennis Banks page 171
2018 Princess Story for Adaea page 172 - 174
2018 Brigid Marlin & Friends - Show in England page 175
2018 Visionary Art Show Moscow – 1st Prize Graphics page 176
2018 Kazuko 50th Anniversay of School – page 177 - 180
2018 Della and Dale visiting Japan page 181
2018 Kanazawabunko. Art Festival 2018 page 182 - 185
2018 Della Storytelling Dream Keys - Japan page 186 - 187
2018 Della sharing Stories/Art for One World /Painting page 188 - 190
2018 Asaba Art Square Events page 191
2018 Great Buddha and Bamboo Garden page 192
2018 Tokyo - Ruu Ruu - La La La- Friend & Beads page 193 - 195
2018 Gifted Children's Pipe page 196
2018 Warrior of the Rainbow .. Rainbow Arch page 197 - 199
Activity Cards - location listed on Activity front page page 200 +
Thank yous / Contributors

Beginnings 1968 - 74

Beginnings come in ususual ways
Adversity brings strength
and new opportunity for fulfilling
your visions for the world
You see your dreams & the Cosmic One
is speaking with a hidden hand
You know you are to travel the world
and being in motion brings magic
Synchronicity is speaking to you
and is welcomed with open arms
and your open heart speaks of an
"All is One" life

"what a sprinkling of magic will do"
1968 Della & Dale fell in love at the Stardust Ballroom.

This book asks many questions that can become a book for you too. In doing the Transformation Map you are to show your problem and solution moments. One question is "where did you first fall in love? For us it was the Stardust Ballroom. Synchronicity was at play when Dale & I met at the "Stardust Ballroom" in Edmonton. What a sprinkling of magic will do to change ones life. Soon after meeting and enjoying dancing at the Peppermint Lodge we decided to go steady. Steady it has been now for 50 years. We moved together to Toronto in 1968 to start our life together. Our main goal was to save money to travel.. and that we did finally flying one way to Rome in 1970 to explore Europe. 2018 is 50 years that we have been together.

Ready to dance!

See the "Journey to the Giant Flower" Card

"travel will open doors" - dream message
1971 -Della & Dale traveled Europe

This book shows Milestones. One part of these are Travel Adventures. The first we had was travelling by Volkswagon Van for one and a half years.and stopped in campsites. We went through France, Austria, Germany, Holland, Greece and Spain. As we traveled I sketched in black & white drawing. One memorable trip was to Morocco where we drove across the desert to Goulamine for a shopkeeper to get him goulamine beads.They were beads originally from Italy made in a Murano glass making technique called millefiori. In gratitude for us getting the beads he gifted us 7 1/2 kilos of beads. The beads were so inspirational and we made many necklace designs that funded our travels further. Some I used in designs I painted.

Dale drives to Goulamine

The shopkeeper in Goulamine

Donkey to the market

Millefiori or thousand flower beads

See the "Make a Necklace" Activity

"You can fly in your Bird Helmet" dream message
1971 Della & Dale travel Europe Setback - Bird Helmet Solution

In writing I made a Transformation Map showing problems and solutions. As we travelled around Europe I continued to sketch in black and white. We had one problem time and I felt the only solution was to go into my inner world. The birds would come to my window to sing. Later I realized this time was "dream incubation" and the blessing is that I, for the first time, started to remember my dreams of astrally travelling to magical places. In a dream I went to the Dream Temple of Asceplius, was gifted a caduceus, and met a merbird and she guided me to hills with a rainbow. I visioned two birds with necks intertwined (with designs from the millefiori beads) I wore. Later I made this into a Bird Helmet to travel to magic lands.

See the "Bird Helmet" Activity Card

"saw book with imaginary birds"
Wrote a poem from a dream called "Freedom" wooden eagle carved fierce & strong in flight - it had a handle for me to grab when
I needed to fly"

1972 - Della teaching Design at Humber College

When back in Canada, I taught Interior Design at a new College called Humber. I took some of my experiences from travelling and since I loved nature so much, created a course on Designing Interiors using Nature as an inspiration. It was part of a a certificate Interior Design Night course that I designed. When I was not teaching I was painting. I showed my paintings in the Humber College Gallery and sold my first painting of the Elemental Dodo in Dodoland.

"In my dream laughed - shook
my head and stars fell out"1973

1972 Health Diagnosis kickstarts Trip to India & "All is One"

While teaching college I had a major health setback I had a cancer diagnosis and knew my life would be different. I was about to have a summer break from teaching and knew intuitively India was the place for me to be. Dale and I were given the names from our travel agent of Aroon & Indur Shivdasani in Bombay. We got a hotel by the Gateway to India from the India on $5 a day but they insisted we stay with them. It became our base as we travelled by trains and buses as far south as we could go, to Bangalore in the middle and Kashmir in the North. It was in Kashmir on a houseboat I had a revelation that all was one. This shaped my life's journey. I wrote and painted what became "Journey to a Lotus". I knew my life would be different and my goal was to make it for all and that is why this book is called Art for One World.

See "Create a Healing Story" Activity

"I am sitting on the lotus but the lotus is in you"
1973 - Della & Dale travel to India

When I started to paint and write "Journey to a Lotus" I was travelling in India. I looked in a lotus flower and thought "this would be a beautiful place for someone to sit". I painted someone and realized later that day it was Buddha. I had a dream of a Cosmic One who said, "Ï am sitting in the lotus but the lotus is in you." I painted this dream as the "Lotus One".

Della on Dal Lake, Kashmir   "Lotus One" from a dream

Tibetan woman - Bead Mentor.   "Inside the lotus" - India

See "Cosmic One" Art Activity

"Everything is Spirit - everything is a gift"
1974 Della & Dale's Second trip to India

The second trip to India we took my brother Murray and we collected unique beads to make into power necklaces that we later showed at a Atrium gallery in Toronto.

Dale in Kasmir in a Tibetan Robe from Tibet.

First time I saw a lotus

We designed necklaces.

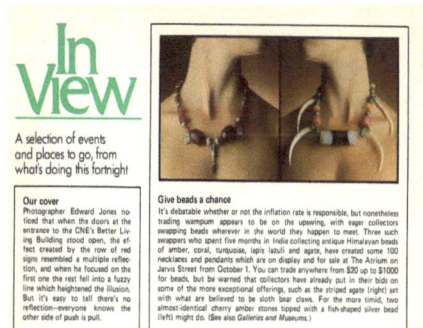

Our necklaces in Toronto Life

See the "Necklace with Beads" Activity Card

"many dreams of the Dodoland Dragon Ship"
Friends became part of Dodoland

While teaching I was also painting Dodoland. I asked friends which fantasy character they would like to become .. we had our faces painted, dressed up in costumes & lived our dreams!

To the right of Dragon Ship is Michael Wesselink (Incredible Red Banana), Below Sal Jo Williams, (Seeing Eye Butterfly), John Mcleod (Dancing Bear), Rainbow, Barney & Tom Williams (Baby Panda) with Rainbow Dolphin and Elemental Dodoland headresses from N.Y.C, Ava Stone (Dancing Flamingo - also painting), Dale (RainbowDolphin) and Della, painting of Banana, George with his first child (Brigadier Smutley), Jeannie Thomas , Bruce (Wise Owl & Wonder Walrus), Loosie Parres (Oh La La Giraffe), & Virgil Scott (Half Past Seven Beaver),

Beginnings - Kazuko Asaba

On the other side of the world - in Japan Kazuko Asaba is also starting something wonderful - a new Art School for children and does imaginative masks, costumes & art. She also catches the "travel bug" and first goes to the Pacific Ocean University and travels and learns. After she travels on a 111 day voyage with her 3 year old son to Europe. She is inspired by two people - Erva Farnsworth and Ruth Asawa.

1970 Japanese students from the Art School made 100 masks /costumes

Kazuko encourages the children to use their imaginations and the masks were made in paper maiche. Kazuko was inspired by seeing paper maiche in Mexico.

Kazuko travels to San Francisco in 1970 & Europe with her son in 1973

For her first trip to San Franciso Kazuko was at the Pacific Ocean University. Her classroom was traveling. When in San Francisco, her girlfriend introduced her to Erva Farnsworth. She was a teacher, loved taking photos, and over many years helped Kazuko. Another important trip was her 111 day trip to she made with her son Dan to travel to Europe. They stay in homes to have a more everyday experience. This influenced her later in life as she had many exchange students.

Erva Farnsworth

Travel Europe with Dan

At Gaudi's Park in Barcelona

1979 - Kazuko's Transformed - India's Nek Chand Rock Garden.

When Kazuko travels to India and San Francisco she is transformed and her convictions to use art to understand other cultures and bring the community is strengthened.
Kauzko found it to be very transformative to visit India. She saw the Nek Chad Rock Garden which had been created not from real events but from dreams. Nek Chand Saini was a self-taught Indian artist, known for building the Rock Garden of Chandigarh, an eighteen-acre sculpture garden in the city of Chandigarh, India. This was an inspiration as was meeting Ruth Asawa in San Fancisco.

Trip to San Francisco again

Kazuko won a ticket for San Francisco in a rollerskating contest. She was happy to be in San Francisco again. Kazuko met Ruth Asawa, a teacher and sculptor, who was an inspiration. She had a large family and still had time to do art with others. This was the time of the Viet Nam war and a lot of people were under stress. Ruth felt when the mind was traumatized you can change the heart through art. It can be healing. The power of art to change ways. She was an art education advocate. In 1968 she started the Alverdo School and started with no money and making art from throw away object, using "bread clay" to sculpt and encouraging hands - on art. She believed artists should teach the children. She had such an intrumental role in the art community that she was honored to have the San Francisco Art School named after her.

Photo - Cunnigham Trust

at David Zwirner Gallery

Photo Greta Michell

Della & Dales Transformation Cycle 1975-81

Birth Dream Cycle 1975 – 1981
"Birth" painting – oil and egg tempera 2013

Divinely limited in body but Dreams bring Transformation
As Dodoland is published Caterpillars change to Butterflies
You visit the Cosmic Lotus One with Chakra Lotuses inside
Where there is a ring of Rainbow Light on your finger
You record it on a Dream Wheel and visit Wandering Spirit
In a teepee you write the "Magical Earth Secrets"
Rainbow Dolphin transforms to Power Bird - White Eagle
Together we enjoy a Symposium for Humanity
Rainbow Rose Festival brings Mystical opportunities

"You can be whatever your imagination wants"
1976 Dodoland - Our Own Studio Gallery Mirvish Village Toronto

Ed Mirvish rented studios to artists on Markham St. in Toronto. I rented a studio and this is where I first painted "Dodoland". In the house there was a gallery called Our Own Studio and here I had my first show. Dodoland was the land I astrally travelled to in my dreams.

"Travelling to the moon"

"Neptune - Crystal Cup"

"Elemental Dodo"

"Journey to Giant Flowers"

Dale as Rainbow Dolphin

"Bananas - (Michael)"

See the "Story Map for Imaginary Story" activity

"Dream Wheels as a moving picture with words".

1976 - Creation of Dream Wheel

Decided to make in 1976 a Dream Wheel showing my dreams. I looked at my Dream Diary and wrote the most important creative dreams that showed inner growth or creative ideas for my future work. In the middle of the wheel, I put real life events such as getting together with family or going to a show and on the outer wheel the dreams in a short one line nutshell title and then in the middle wheel a drawing of the dream and a sketch that would jog my dream memory. I said to myself after 30 years I would share this with the world. After 2010 I started to write the Dream Wheels book. It is about the 36 Dream wheels and how they have been manifested into books, writings, plays and lots of art for the world. The book was published in 2013.

See " Make a Dream Wheel" Activity

"Dale was with a white deer in my dream"
1977 - Dale & Della visit Japan

I always had a love of the way the Japanese people had different parts of their lives as art, like food, and clothes and painting and architecture -- so I wanted to go to Japan before finishing the paintings for Dodoland. We went to many beautiful temples in Kyoto and visited the ancient capital of Nara where I saw many deer. I painted a Fawn Forest with white deer for the Dancing Flamingo part of Dodoland and her home had a pattern from a kimono on it.

See the "Travel Adventure" Activity

"the body is a temple"
1976 - "Japanese symbols have energy"

1977 Visiting Kyoto & Osaka

Della (I) and Dale visited many sacred temples and Rock Gardens in Kyoto and see the Bunraku in Osaka. Unforgettable moments.

"The Bird Helmet is the way to travel"
1977 - "Journey to Dodoland" published in Los Angles

Doug Riseborough made an introduction to Dr. Dick Mazurek who published a large format book of Dodoland. Dodo Land is to encourage creativity & build confidence. Della had a dream of her Bird Helmet on fire like a Phoenix Bird when in New York after the book was published and suggested the books be given to the poorest children - 6000 were gifted at Christmas 1978 to the underprivileged The book won the Printers Institute of America award for best Graphic Art in 1978. Paul Showalter - book design.

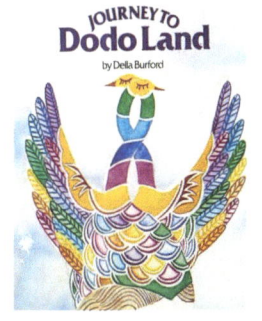
Dodoland Book

Dragon Ship

Dale & Doug

Dodoland Map

Dr. Dick Mazurek

See "Imaginary Map", & "Bird Helmet" Activity

"dream with the Rainbow Dolphin"
Celebration in Acton

We became friends with Sal - Jo & Tom Williams in 1970 and watched their four children grow. When Dodoland was published we had a celebration for the book at Acton. Their house in Acton was my home in Dodoland.

Sal - Jo Williams above and Tom Williams below.

"My mum told me in a dream to not be as literal"

1977 Mum & Dad make Bird Helmet

My mum and dad, knowing how important the Bird Helmet was to me, and that it came from a dream, created a Bird Helmet for me to wear for storytelling. My dad, being an engineer, constructed it with copper wire and my mother, an artist, added feathers.

"the flowers are beauty & enchantment"

1977 - Giant Flower Island

Many projects were done around the Giant Flower Islands which is part of Dodoland and are macro-photographs by Dale Bertrand. The flowers show the beauty of our earth. The children pretend they are large and you can climb in them and see new things and hear music. The deeper you go the more beautiful it becomes.

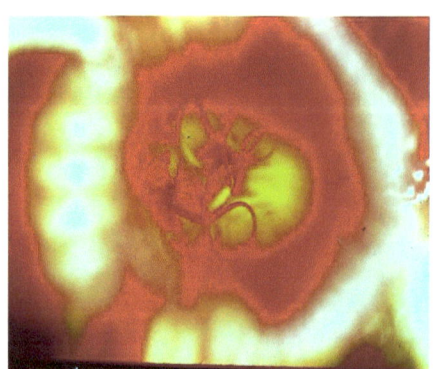

See the "Journey to the Flowers" Activity

"As caterpillar changes to a butterfly, you can fly"

1978 - Symposium for Humanity L.A.

Dale and I lead a Dodoland children's workshop. We were able to connect with some of the Presenters like Buckminster Fuller, Yogi Bhajan, Elizabeth Kubler Ross, Patricia Sun and Swami Sachinanda. There was Activists, Artist & Exhibitors. I met the Butterfly Lady (Dr. Stevanne Auerbach) as I saw lights flashing from her Butterfly Mask - I went to talk to her - it felt meant to be. We paraded & presented and shouted **"love the planet, save the planet"**. The group was well ahead of its time. In 2018 Stevanne published a book to help Save the butterflies. - "My Butterfly Collection - On the wings of the Butterfly"

Many butterfly authors: Della Burford, Dr. Stevanne Auerbach, Marcus Bach & Trina Paulus

Rainbow Caterpillar - painted - Star Rainbow - kids joined

"some things are meant to be"
1979 - Symposium - Rainbow Rose - Los Angles - Mystical Vision Brings New Opportunity

We attended the Rainbow Rose Symposium and led Dodoland workshops for the children. Dale was waiting to see a healer, Dr. David Davies, as he had lost his hearing in his left ear. As he waited he went into a session by an English healer - Rose Gladden. She went into a trance and in her time and space he saw an Ancient Being who said he (Dale) would be involved in a path of healing. He felt after that he must study druid teachings and as synchronicity has it when he visited his mum, 5 days later, she gifted him ancient manuscripts written at the turn of the century by a man called John Hugh Roberts. He later produced books of illuminations of some manuscripts.

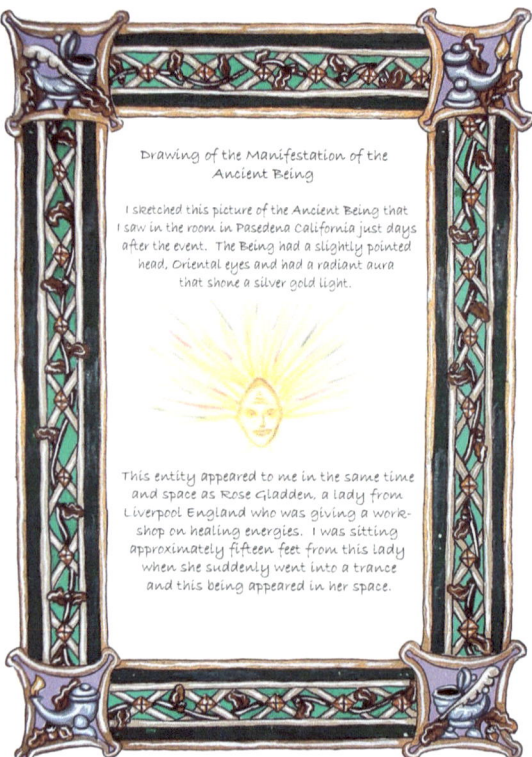

Ancient manuscripts

Illuminations made later

See the "Cosmic One" Activity

"You are in the center of the Medicine Wheel and it is turning around you"

1979 - Project at Wandering Spirit Survival School - Toronto

I (Della) lead various art projects over a four year period with the students at the School run by Vern Harper and Pauline Shirt. Each morning they had a sweetgrass ceremony at the school. The children made a Mural of Magical Earth Secrets which had come in a dream to Della when she woke up with a rainbow on her finger. Della lead Painting, Tedrian movement and Dale, a Medicine Mural that were taken to be shared at a Conference in Sweden. This was a Ontario Art Council & Inner City Angel project.

Painting a Magical Earth Secrets Mural

Vern Harper & Della Burford

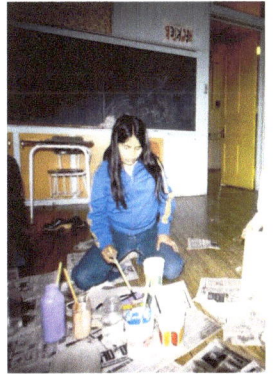

Luanna Harper painting

Mural project with Dale Bertrand

"See the "Nature Wish" Activity card

"The birds are god's instruments"
1980 -Kootenay Annual Fair Amanda's Birthday

In 1977, I was told in a dream to paint Magical Earth Secrets in this special place called the Kootenay. We spent each summers in the Kootenay Valley..the people and children were so special and the place magical. Here my sister introduced me to the man who made Dodoland possible. Here is a birthday party of a special little girl who lives there - Amanda Erickson. The children heard Dodoland and made Bird Helmets.

See "Make a Bird Helmet"

"Elisa is moving around the Medicine Wheel"
1981 Performance at Easalen

Big Sur - thrilled to be invited to perform Dodoland at Easalen. One of the teachers, Elisa Lodge, was one of my best friends in Los Angeles when the book Dodoland was being published. At Easalen she performed the Dancing Flamingo. We have kept in touch and loved to see her recently in her 80's still dancing a Butterfly dance. She is an inspiration for many as was our Producer Tedrian Chizik shown here sitting with a child.

See "Metamorphosis" Activity

"Story or Dance in front of paintings/photos"
1980 - Dodoland performed at Museums, Hospitals & Schools in New York City

In integrating the work into the world my dream of dancing in front of the images was incorporated. We felt honored to have performances at - Museo del Barrio, Museum of Natural History, Sloan Kettering Hospital, and a Teachers Workshop at Columbia University. We had a performance at the Cuban Refugee Camps.

Della's with Tedrian Chizik, Jerry Schrair, & Diane Godford

Museum of Natural History

Merian Soto as Flamingo,

Cuban Refugee Camp

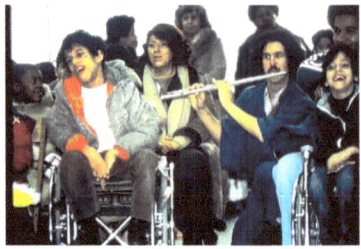

Jerry Schrair - Museo del Barrio

See the "Bird Helmet" Activity

"Some symbols have special energy"
1980 - Mystical Painting of Symbols

I had two mystical experiences with symbols. In the late 70's I did a painting for a yoga center of the sacred Om as I said I would paint it in color. They gave me a photo of their guru - Swami Sivananda to put beside me. I asked for guidance as I painted. Something mystical happened because as I painted a light shone from the OM. If I used the wrong color the light would not shine. I felt I was co-creating with the divine. I put Om in all the characters when I was painting Magical Earth Secrets.
I also saw a symbol in a book that I was attracted to -- painted it in a painting in meditation. Thirty- five years later, when studying Dream Yoga with Tenzin Rinpoche, I discovered it was the HUNG symbol they used to open the Heart Chakra for Heart presence in dreams.

"Search for the Seed" by Della Burford

See "Cosmic One" Activity

Medicine Ways - Kazuko Asaba

Kazuko travelled to Egypt and found the history and energy fascinating, peaceful, spiritual and full of good medicine. She had her first trip to Egypt in 1984. She went to the Great hall and burial chamber of King Khufu and since she was alone laid down and felt great power. She organized a Cultural Exchange for Japanese students to go to Egypt in 1989. She went to Egypt 18 times.

1982 California- San Francisco

Kazuko went back to San Francisco. In San Francisco she was very inspired when she experienced an Art Festival and in Los Angeles a multi- cultural community. These both greatly influenced her decision of what she wanted to do in her life.

1983 -Asaba Art School projects

The Asaba Art School students created a Bird Land and Fruit & Vegetable Land. For special concerts they often explored themes like birds, vegetables & fruits, Egypt or the universe.

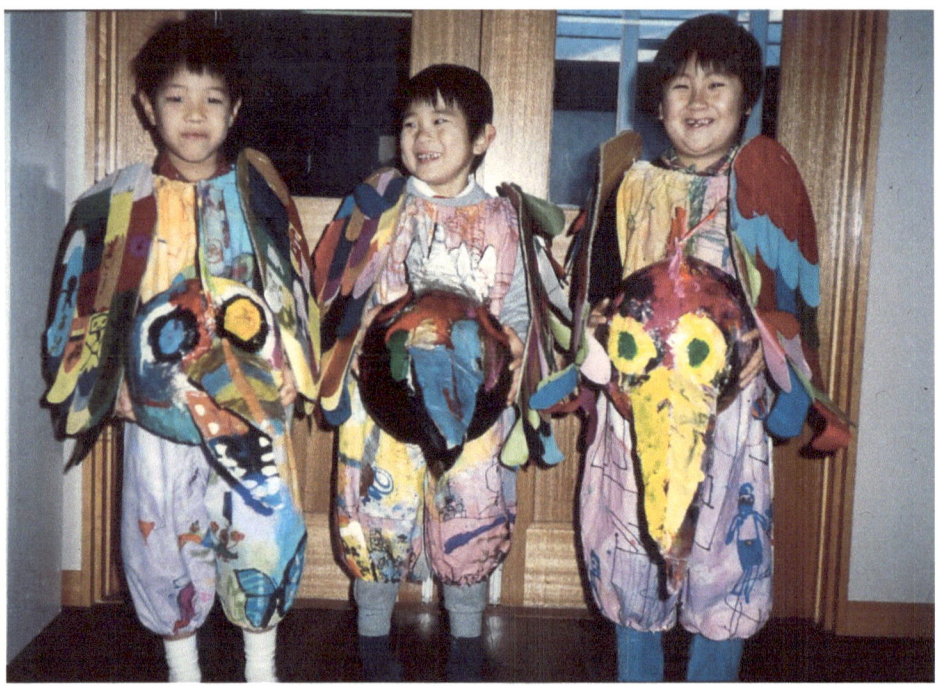

1985 The Goddess Nuit's Influence

Kazuko was very influenced by the Goddess Nuit in Egyptian Mythology. She strongly related to her energy and how she represented the the sun rising and making each day new again. One of her students was having a struggle and she took him each day for six months to see the sunrise.

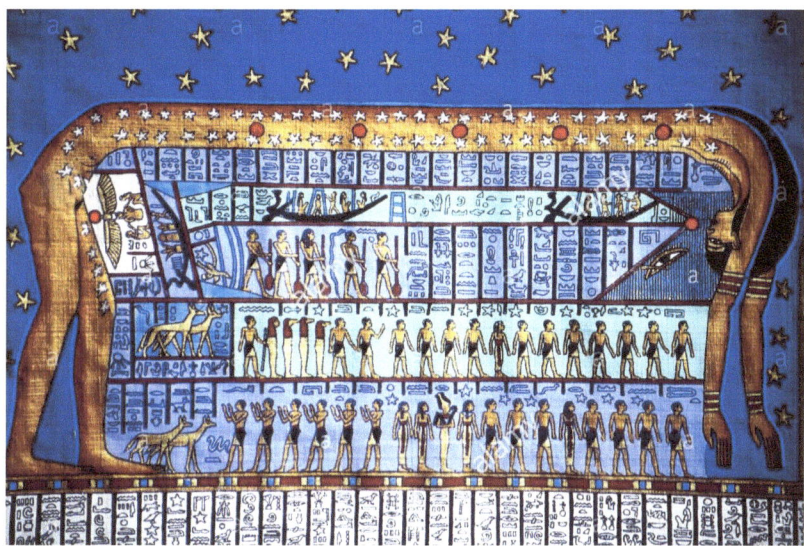

1984 Japanese students at Art Exhibition in Luxor, Egypt

Kazuko's love and passion for Egypt was fulfilled by her going to Egypt many times. She worked with her students on many themes with the mythology of Egypt. Some were exhibited in Egypt.

1985 - Social problem - Child Suicide

(Written while in the 4th grade of elementary school)
(Extract written on February 1985 while in 5th grade of elementary school, one day before his passing away)

Exam Wars

Exam sheets were handed out
Total silence filled the room
The exam war had been declared
Armed with missiles instead of pencils
With erasers instead of machine guns
The exam sheets in front of us were our foes
Filling them out with knowledge earned
through hardships and efforts
This war ends when we finish this exam
Winning brings us joy but losing leaves us with anxiety
taking place of wounds
Exam wars are strenuous and painful wars which cause
changes in our lives
(Written while in the 4th grade of elementary school)

As schools are things made by humans, people tend to think they are requisites, however the question lies in whether going to school will make us happy. We are made to advance, step by step, to higher levels in the school system. So what's the deal in being hired by a major corporation and eventually becoming its CEO? The answer is we simply become old, our capabilities slow down with age, so what is the fun in running a business? We would become rich but would be at a loss in what to do. There were no schools in the old days and people lived freely. The issue here is progress. If there were no schools there would neither be progress nor the need for money. I think we have had enough progress. I think it's useless for me to further elaborate on this - Translated by Nick Muhrin

Kazuko changes her Vision

This poem was written by a students in 1985. Kazuko was shaken and wanted to let the author know she heard what he had to say. She felt the impact so deeply it changed the direction of her life's work and she went many times to Egypt and she found a spiritual way and the peace helped her. She vowed to make her program more spiritual, creative and a happy experience.

1988 - Celebration - 20th Anniversary of Art School - Nagahama Hall

For the 20th Anniversary of the Art School, at the Nagahama Hall, students made Body Rainbow cushions. Also an educational book by Kazuko was published - "Magical Studio".

See "Dancing Body Rainbows" (Cushions)

Della & Dale's Medicine Ways
1982 -1988

In your Dreams you find Medicine Ways
A place of New Growth with Dream Birds & Power Allies
Dale visit ancient sites in Wales, on his Merlin journey.
The synchronicity of finding the Stone Book of Knowledge
is to be honored.. bringing more trips on the Druid Quest
As Dodoland is performed in Gautemala, New York & D.C.
In dreams Elder Bear People dance in a circle
And On the Medicine Wheel the Eagle Child guides you
Good medicine is shared with people everywhere
In dreams the Mother of the World praises the Light

"Look into your dreams and you will find more about who you are!" -dream message

1981 - Inner City Angels - Toronto Project Opportunidad - Harlem

Della led workshops thru the Inner City Angels in Art and Storytelling for 17 years while she freelanced as an artist - this included Dodoland, and Magical Earth Secrets. At the same time the group in New York took the Dodoland & Magical Earth Secrets show around to all East Harlem schools. We had a costume and drama project at many schools in New York.

Inner City Angels project

Storyteller performing Della

P.S. 9 New York

Children in Harlem wearing Bird Helmet

See the " Story for Imaginary Picture Book" Activity

"You will go on a Merlin journey"
1981- Dale trip to Wales

When Dale received the manuscripts, he gave a copy to Dr. David Davies, professor Emeritius, from Abergavanny Wales. A year later he went to Wales to meet with Dr Davies. Dale was to initiate the 'Mountain Peace Pipe', he had been given and chose Ysgyryd Fawr, to do his ceremonial Peace Pipe. Having been driven out to the mountain in David's Morris Minor, David's last words to Dale as he started his trip up the mountain, was, with his arm extended out the window, he shouted "Excalibur", that was the last time they saw each other. Dale followed the pathway up the mountain until he found the likely spot he had been told about of an ancient Druidic Cave and proceeded to do his pipe ceremony there. A magical moment with the clouds banking up and curling over the east side of the mountain while the west over the Brecon Hills were in blue sky.

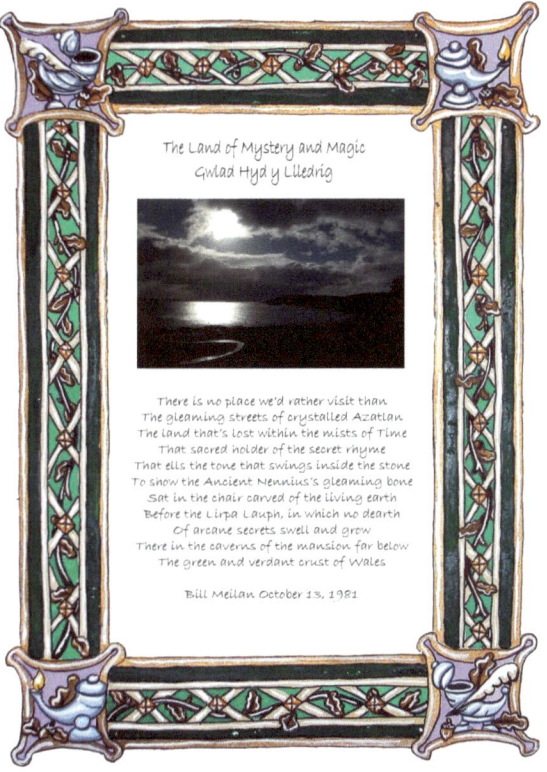

See the Travel Adventure" Activity

"In Dodoland you have the depth of the earth but light and freedom" - dream message

1982 - "Magic in me" Dodoland performed in Guatemala City

Dodoland was one of the Feature Events at this large Symposium for teachers from Latin & South American, who worked with physically- challenged children -"Magic in Me" We taught the integration of the Arts Music, Art & Drama and had Dodoland performances at the National Theatre in Gautemala City. Many teachers lined up for hours afterwards to get into the workshop as it was known as being fun. After Dale and I (Della) visited the sacred site of Tikal.

Teacher's Workshop

The cast with Miss Guatemala

"In Dodoland you live your dream"

Receiving a Bird Helmet

"Make a Bird Helmet"(Gautemalans called - Quetzal Hat)

"Now is the time to dance on the Medicine Wheel"
1982 - American Indian Community Centre - New York

We had a performance of Dodoland on a Medicine Wheels painted on the floor of the American Community Centre which has been serving the Indigenous community in N.Y.C since 1969.

We were thrilled that a member of the community who was one hundred years old came to the show!

Tedrian as Elemental Dodo dancing on Medicine Wheel

Banana Man in this performance became the trickster.

Ray Evans Harrell - the Medicine Wheel was painted"by Mary Big Horse's husband Al for the Production of Quetzalcoatl

See the "Four Winds - Four Directions Activity

"Told must go on vision quest - to stay overnight on Kootney Plains." We were guided by a mentor.

1982 - Vision Quest - Kootenay

Dale and I went on a Vision Quest in the Kootenay Plains. I had my Bird Helmet. It was a full moon night and we were in white birches. I meditated and made a fire. I heard a noise ahead and saw that a brown bear was coming toward me. I remembered our mentor had said if a bear came when I was painting to tell him how good he looks. I did this and he did look good as his coat was shiny. Then I put on my Bird Helmet, rang my tibetan bells, & stood up and said, "Let's be at Peace." The bear turned and went the other way. When it was over, then I felt afraid and went with bells ringing to where Dale was doing his quest.

Dale at a Vision Quest
The painting on the left - after quest - a Elder Bear dance, eagle cries, unicorn, Deer Shaman Prophet, mermaid, Merlin, Tikal, & the Mother of the World

Medicine Ways - Della Burford

See the "Four winds - Four directions Activity

"please make our world a peaceful place"

1982 Ceremony for Peace

We were part of many ceremonies for Peace. Here I wore ceremonial gear - a Rainbow outfit from Gautemala. My hat was made by a Shaman as was Dale's Buffalo headdress. We focused our energy for peace and love to be in our world.

"I and the earth are one, I love the earth
I will protect the earth" -
message from the Magical Earth Secrets

See the "Nature Wish Mural" Activity

"Thoughts create energy" - dream message

1982 - Dodoland at St. Peter's Cathedral - Citycorp - New York

Before the show was to start, children filed in from the United Nations School all dressed in costumes and wearing their Bird Helmets to go to Dodoland. This filled my heart. We always formed a circle before the show to show our connection to each other and together gave the intent to bring love to the children and encouragement in "being what they wanted to be".

Children filed in from the United Nations School

Lotus One   Citycorp theatre in the round

See the "Bird Helmet" Activity

"Antiques are a reuse and recycle solution"
Dale - Communications Manager Harbourfront Antique Mkt - Toronto

Dale spent 4 years as Communication Manager at the Harbourfront Antique Market in Toronto. It had upwards of 240 dealers on the weekend and was a hive of activity. His personal love of antiques was from both his mum who loved to go out and find a bargain and my (Della's) mum who had an antique store called Fireside Antiques. Shadflyguy describes the market online in an article from 2016 - " When we started in the early 80's the market would be held on about an acre of parkland near the terminal building, with the 100 or so vendors being set up in parking lots and green spaces right alongside the water. In the winter we could go across the road and inside an old one story warehouse. These were the glory days.
It's hard to imagine now just how "hot" the market was."

Reusing, recycling and reconstituting are important.

"If things are open it will be more fun"
1983 - Dodoland at the Smithsonian Institute in Washington D.C.

The show was to encourage creativity and build confidence to know we can live our dreams. This show was the only Dodoland show where a woman who played the harp was one of the musicians. The show was improv and had participation from the audience.

See "Magical Earth Cosumes/PlayActivity

"You are sitting in the Medicine Wheel"
1983 - Dodoland Program in Ontario's Hearing Impaired Schools

Wintario sponsored programs in the three hearing impaired Schools in Ontario. The teachers when we arrived said we would be disappointed - we were the opposite as the children were so creative and came alive. Myself (Della) and Dale did Ocean Painting, Body Energy Rainbows, & Storytelling. Movement was with Merian Soto & Tedrian Chizik. Alice Brownlee collaborated in all parts and did signing.

Alice Brownlee (Jerome) who signed for our project with two students.

This is a teacher & student signing what is in the Body Rainbow

See the "Body Energy Rainbow" Activity

"Dreaming on the Medicine Wheel"
"In dreams changing colors, shapes & form."

1983 - Dodoland - Teaching Dreams at Christie St. School - Toronto

I (Della) have made a Wheel of Dreams - Dream Mandala since 1976 each year. In this project I encouraged the children to write and paint from their dreams and encouraged "honoring dreams" by making art about them.

See "Make a Dream Wheel" Activity

"You are the one who opens the doors"
1983 Della at Sunnyview School

All the children were in wheelchairs. They were carefully lifted out of the chairs and traced around their bodies - then they added colors and symbols. The boy on the right said "lets have an art show" so all the children's art was collected and filled the walls of the school.

Della looking at the Dodoland map with children from Sunnyview School

See the "Body Energy Rainbow" Activity

"I was to do a painting of the Singing Tree"
1984 Trip to Peru

Dale traveled to Peru to research for this Celtic project. He photographed from the highest places he could climb to in Macchu Picchu. Huayna Picchu - most photographers don't climb to such heights. Producer of our show in New York, Tedrian went also to Peru and visited the Altar of the Sun God
in Macchu Picchu and dedicated the Dodoland story and his project in New York around the story "to the children of the world."

"I had a Mother of the World dream the night I brought the Roerich slides from New York"

1984 Roerich's Painting to Prisoners

I did this project with Shizuye Takashima, whose story "Child in Prison Camp" was performed in Japan at the Ekidan Fuji Theatre Company with 200 performers. Shizuye and myself (Della) worked together on a Peace Project through a group called Peace thru Culture. We took the art of Nicholas Roerich (via slides I had brought from the Roerich Museum in New York) to prisoners at the Toronto Detention Centre. Myself and Shizuye then did art and writing with the women prisoners. One day I worked with some women that were illegal immigrants from Guyana, who were teachers in their own country, One teacher proceeded to read the Dodoland book to me word by word and afterwards told me what a blessing it was for me to come.

Cover of "Child in Prison Camp'

Little Shishan (at left) with playmates at the beginning of WW2.

Della at the Roerich Museum in N.Y.C.

See the Make a Nature Wish Mural Activity

"You find all the pools of water in the desert"

1984- Brooklyn Academy of Music

This show featured projections of Dale's Giant Flower Island photos with the dancers. Everyone went to Dodoland. After the show, I (Della) was requested to go to a class of blind students so they could feel with their hands and with the sense of touch, experience the Bird Helmet. To have the children do this meant so much to me.

See the " Journey to the Giant Flower " Activity

"We - Keepers of Humanities Circle"- Vern Harper
said this to me in a dream message

1985 - Magical Earth Secrets performed in New York

The paintings were done for Magical Earth Secrets and since Dodoland was such a success, the Project Opportunidad New York City chose Della's new story as a play to go to all East Harlem schools. This was before the story was a book.

Make an "Environmental Play" Activity

"Angels are everywhere"
"You have a wishing wand partner"

Angel Sculpture by Pat Brennan

I was honored to be included in the sculptures done by Pat Brennan for her Archangel & Angel series - Pat had a sculpture installation called "Guardians and Archangels From Earth," which has been portraits of friends and aquaintances, each expressed with a mythological theme. "They were real people involved in earthly actions inspired by heavenly ideals". I (Della) was sculpted as one of the angels. Many of the sculptures are of professional dancers. The project was given a grant to tour Russia in 1991.

Della by Pat

3 West Direction - Pat also studied clowning with Richard Pochinko

See "Create your own Healing Story" Activity

"Dreams & Synchronicity should be honored"
1985 - Black Book & Honoring Synchronicity

In 1978 Dale had received 90 Ancient Manuscripts from his mother who inherited them from Charles Steele. They were written by John Hugh Roberts (his grandfather) who wrote before the turn of the century and had a lot of mystical information in them. We were trying to understand them. 7 years later our friends Tom & Sal Williams came from SaltSpring to Toronto where we were living and we picked them up at the airport and they said they had something for Dale. Doug Atkins a mutual friend had found at the Recycling Depot (at the dump) a book written by J.H. Roberts.. Dale was astounded it had been delivered to him 3000 miles.. it was a Black Book which summarized Robert's teachings (that he learned from his grandmother and her 2 friends - 3 Mermaids) that he called The Stone Book of Knowledge. It took years but we honored by action this happening by publishing it in its complete original form in 2014.

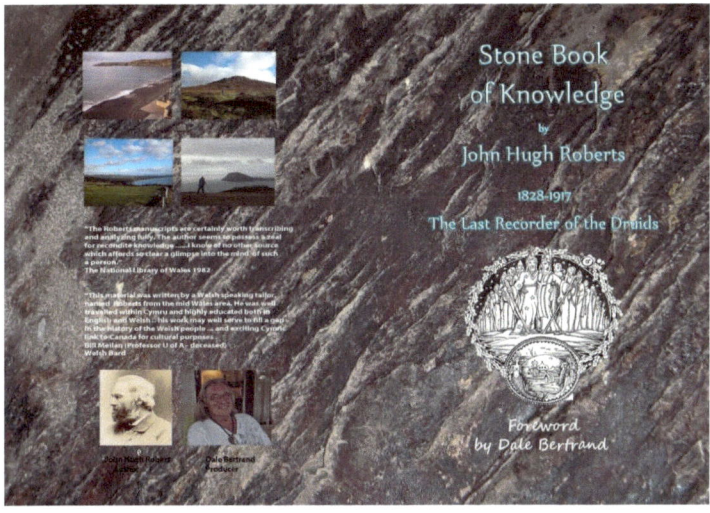

"See "Cosmic One" Activity

"I had a bouquet of paint brushes"

Della and Dale
1987 - Wedding Kootenay

We had a wedding with the special energy of the Kootenay, in the woods with the elves and fairies. We did a special Peace Pipe in a Medicine Wheel Ceremony.

See "Love Wind painting"

" I saw a red bird and sang a Dream Song"
1985 - Painting in the Kootenays

One thing I loved to do when in living in the Kootenay was to paint outside. This is right by the spot where I was when I had the inspiration dream for Magical Earth Secrets and where I did a lot of the paintings.

See the "Ocean Painting" Activity

"had a dream of a Dream Hat for my mum"

1986 - Created a Dream Hat for Desiree from my dream

Much of the guidance on my projects come from dreams. My mother, Desiree, being an artist, encouraged me to paint, dream & be creative. In a dream for her sixty fifth birthday I saw a hat for her. I honored her & my dream by making it! I'll never forget her smile. We showed our paintings together in 1990 when Magical Earth Secrets was performed in Edmonton by Maria Formolo.

"Make a "Dream Wheel Activity"

"dream - my ancestors were in charge of flying"

1986 Trip to Wales - Dale with Bill & Patricia Meilen

Dale went to Wales with Bill and Patricia Meilen. Dale was most fascinated with Bardsey Island and photograhed it from the opposite shore. 10,000 saints are suppose to be buried there. We feel it correlates with Teman written in the manuscripts. This page is from the Book in which Dale shows photos and explains his travels, called "Druidical Quest" which also has photos of some of the original writings.

The mystical Isle of Bardsley.

Illustration from the Stone Book of Knowledge showing Teman

See the "Travel Adventure" Activity

"With this child you will be born" & "masks are transformational" - dream messages

1986 - Studied Baby Clown with Richard Pochinko

I felt privileged to have a chance to work with such an inspired man. Richard helped people go inside themselves to find their uniqueness by moving in the four directions with masks. The masks were made with the eyes shut. I had many dreams during the process. What was birthed was a baby clown. I wrote a diary when doing this and included it in the book I worked on with Dale and Ian Wallace - **Richard Pochinko - Clown thru Mask.**

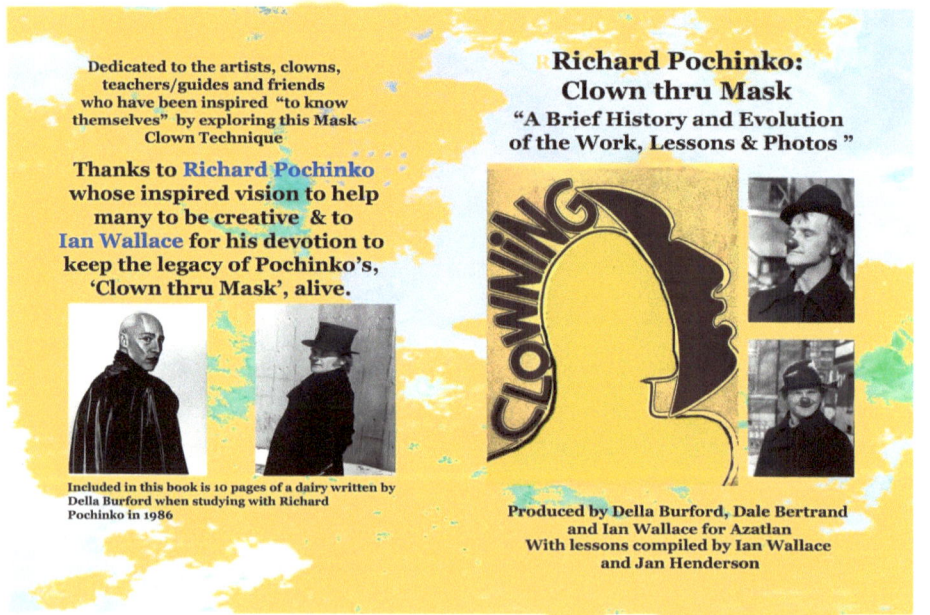

"Make your own Picture Book or Puppet"
1987- Inner City Angels & Ontario Arts Council Projects & Canada Council Reading Program

I (Della) continued my workshops with the Inner City Angels sometimes seeing 300 children a week. My twin sister Donna made puppets. I also did a Reading program with the Canada Council. Dale in 1987 also started "Medicine Wheels projects with the Inner City Angels part-time.

Storytellings & Readings

Twin Donna made puppets

Dale's Medicine Wheel project

I arrived to a school and they had made a large Eagle Child in the hall out of colored tissue.

See "Enviro- Puppets" & "Four Winds/Four Directions"

"it is the dawning of care, share and blessings"
1987 - Cape Cod Writer's /Designing

This was the year of the Harmonic Convergence and many people world-wide were meditating for peace. My students at the Cape Cod Writer's Conference created characters and stories that had a peaceful solution. After this conference we met Julie Lieberman for a peace ceremony. We did it on the mandala I painted for Magical Earth Secrets. This year I also designed and worked with Norah on a line of clothing called Desiree with Lynne Tyrell. They were beautiful silks which were hand woven in Thailand with hand painted sections. Lynne did the designs. She was an incredible storyteller and fun to be with.

Della -Cape Cod Writer's Conference

Lynne Tyrell at Brazilian Ball

Photo Lynne 92 years old

See a "Story Map for Enviro- Picture Book"

"I woke up with a ring of light on my finger and wrote the outline for Magical Earth Secrets"

1987- Dedication Gift of Rainbow

I had been working for years on the Magical Earth Secrets story and finally one night woke to write a dedication at the front of the story, "for nine months I have asked the creator that this gift of the Rainbow be given to you" I saw a small bird in a womb-like enclosure pecking to get out. The next morning to my surprise, my friend Sal said she was having birth signals and was going to the hospital. I did not tell her my dream. We looked after their house. That night was thunder and lightning like we had never experienced before. The next day she came home with a baby boy and Tom and Sal announced that they had chosen the name "Rainbow". They did not know my dream I had the night before and chose the name on their own. Two of their children Barney and Rainbow are our Godsons and we feel privileged. Love to all of the William's family!

Rainbow holding the puppet of Rainbow wings made by Noreen Crone Findlay for the Edmonton Show of Magical Earth Secrets. There are other members of the William's family in the photo. Della on Right with Eagle Child.

See "Make a Enviro -Puppets" Activity

"Every person, country, idea is a petal on a flower"
1988 - Globetree Sweden

I (Della) was honored to be invited to the Globetree Conference in Sweden. The question asked at the conference was - What is of life importance for the future? 600 children & young persons from all over the world responded to the question with drama, dance, poetry, visual art and songs at the Concert Hall in Sweden. Children narrated the Magical Earth Secrets. A native girl from Canada, Karin - Pauline Shirt's niece danced the Eagle Child. Thanks too all of those people in Sweden organizing including Kajsa Dahlstom, Ben Van Brockhorst, Sam Samuelsson & Peroy Kirchner. The words 'Take Care of the Earth' in the chant used in Magical Earth Secrets came to me sitting the front row of the Concert Hall in Stockholm.

Children telling my story were represented from Sweden, South America, Africa, and two Canadians. Karin and the The youngest child was Evan Clifford who was there with his father Neil Clifford. (His grandmother is Karin Clifford)

"Make an Enviro- Hero/Heroine Helper" Activity

Wonder Cycle - Kazuko
1989 - 1995

Kazuko showed her love for other countries by having in 1989 a Cultural Exchange with both Egypt and Turkey with Japanese students. She met Della Burford's book at a ecology Exhibition in Los Angeles and was inspired by it and did art in her school around the book. She took Japanese children to Pueblos in New Mexico sharing her love and wonder of that area and had them share their cultures with each other.

1989- Japan - Egypt Cultural Exchange.

The students study mythology and paint a wall painting. It is a mural in preparation for going to Egypt.

Children doing Wall Painting before their trip to Egypt.

See "Egyptian Story Mural" Activity

1989 Japanese children visit Egypt for Cultural Exchange

The Japanese children visited Egypt and learned and experienced another culture. They visited the Hahraneiya art school in Cairo. They could not speak through their language but did learn that they could speak through their hearts and eyes and understand each other.

1989 - Kazuko - Cultural Exchange with Turkey

Japanese children visited Turkey. The students explained about the Japanese culture and learned about the Turkish culture. This was new to all of them and each day their eyes were open more on how life is in our world.

"There would be crowns of dreams.. crowns for the future" 1990

1991 - Kazuko meets Della Burford's book Magical Earth Secrets

Kazuko met Della Burford's book at an Eco Fair in Los Angeles. Erva Farnsworth bought Kazuko a ticket to go to the Fair. The publisher Western Canada Wilderness Committe in Vancouver went to L.A. and were represented with Sue Fox and her team and Kazuko found the book. It was inspirational and she used it in her program and later spearheaded it with Ruu*Ruu into a play in Japan.

1992 - Kazuko - Kimono and Kachina making in Taos Pueblo

Two cultures on different sides of the world share making something special to them. The Japanese kimonos which they made from sheets that were there and they tiedyed them, and Taos children tried them on to see how they felt, and the people from Pueblo made cardboard Mask Kachinas to show the Japanese children .

1992 - Pueblo Children's Art & Dance

Children at the San Culara Pueblo made a Batik hanging.
They also did a Corn Dance to celebrate the harvest.

1993 Japanese children visit the Northern Pueblo

The Japanese children and Pueblo children share their culture, food and friendship when the Japanese children visit the Pueblo. Swimming in the river was one of their favourite activities.

1993-1994 The Pueblo children learn about the Japanese language.

The children from Pueblo were fascinated by the Japanese language. Since the children did not speak each others language they spoke by their facial and body movement,

1994 - Pueblo children visit Japan (Kyoto).

This year the Pueblo children came to experience the culture of Japan. The Pueblo people had fantastic costumes and shared their customs and ways and the Japanese children shared their culture.

Intuitive Cycle - Kazuko

In 1998 Kazuko visited the Japanese Ainu tribe in Hokkaido who are a very intuitive people. For the 30th Anniversary event at Yokohama she presented Della's book as a children's play called "Majical Rainbow". In 1999 there was the first Kanzawa-bunko Festival which has become a tradition each year.

Ainu Tribe from Hokkaido

Iroquois Prayer

This beautiful Iroquois prayer is used by Kazuko at the beginning and end of gatherings in Japan.

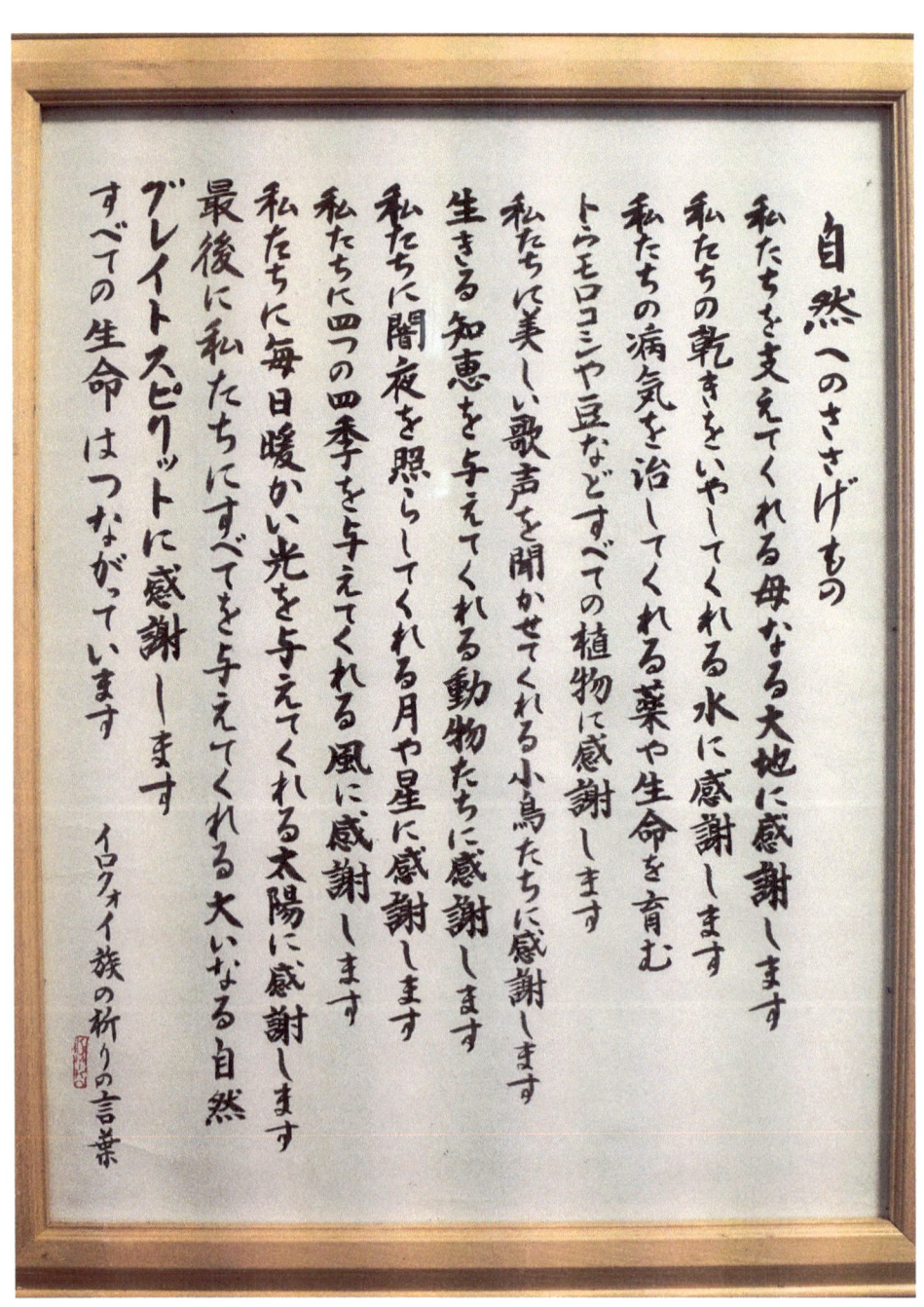

1998 Kazuko's class does Magical Rainbow play from Della's book

To celebrate the 30 Year Anniversary of the art school they put on a play at Nagahama Hall in Kanazawabunko.

See the "Rainbow Hat" Activity

1998- Kazuko's visit to the Japanese Ainu Tribe - Hokkaido

The intuitive and spiritual ways of the Ainu resonated with Kazuko and she incorporated an Indigenous Plaza as part of the Kanzawabunko Festival.

1999 - First Kanazawabunko Festival

In seeing Art Festivals in San Francisco Kazuko knew she wanted to create an event to feature art and entertainment, and with a "love the earth" theme. The first Festival was at the Syomyoji Temple. This is a Buddhist Temple in a quiet area with a rich history. As the Festivel grew the theme reflected the needs of the children and the planet. Children's Future is Earth's Future - Earth's Future is Children's Future.

Della and Dale's Wonder Cycle 1989 - 1995

Wonder Dream Cycle 1989 - 1995
"Wonder" painting is egg tempera and acrylic washes 2013

In your Dreams you find Wonder
A place where Inner Space is as powerful as Outer Space
You are told everyone has a Spirit Horse & and mine is Unicorn
The Tibetan Wind Horse is the essence of yourself
You echo the love & wonder of nature in Magical Earth Secrets
published it reaches many and is performed in a Dream Dance
Rainbow Wing puppet rules and is included with Dodoland
Online for millions to see. In dreams you are told to
Manifest Art to Beauty. Dale has visited Sacred Peruvian Sites
Also enters the inner pyramid of Chitza Itza.

"Everyone has their own power animal"
1989 - Storytelling Project with David Lertzman -Toronto

When the Magical Earth Secrets was published, Paul George from Western Canada Wilderness Commitee who spearheaded the publication, said he had heard the story told by David and loved it. Della and David collaborated on many events together combining story and music telling the Magical Earth Secrets.

See the "Four Winds - Four Directions "Activity

"You must paint when the vision come easily"
1990 - Magical Earth Secrets Western Canada Wilderness Committee

Foreword: "Della Burford reminds us we need a vision and that with the help of our children we can develop new and creative ways to take care of the environment".
Tom Lyons. - Education for a Global Perspective
"As you soar along with Rainbow Wings, you and your child will learn that it will take each and everyone's small effort to get us there.. Children of the world need hope not despair. This book and your positive actions provide it".. **Dr David Suzuki**

Book launch for Magical Earth Secrets

Paul George, Adrian Carr & Della Burford designing .

As synchronity has it, Sue Fox on the right, Magical Earth Secrets to an Eco-Fair in 1990 to Los Angeles.. this happened to be where Kazuko saw it and purchased it to take back to Japan. Della visited Sue in 2018 and took her photo. after her & Dale saw the story performed in Japan.

"You can dance to tell a story"
1991 - Maria Formolo Dance Co. performs Magical Earth Secrets

After seeing my (Della's) story "Magical Earth Secrets" told in a teepee, Maria decided to produce the story as a Dance and have an Environmental Event. Myself and my mother, Desiree, had a collaborative show of our paintings in the lobby. Maria danced, Noreen Crone Findlay made and worked the Eagle child puppet, and Pauline Lebell sang. The production was like a dream.

See the "Enviro-Puppet" Activity

"There are layers of children"
1992 Friends of the Environment Edmonton Writer in Residence

Dale and I led many workshops in Toronto including TD's 'Friends of the Environment'. Protecting the environment was a major part of our work. I was also part of the Writer in Residence in Edmonton and at one school, Earl Buxton went each year for four years to work with the new second graders to do books.

Environmental Posters at West Preparatory School

"Make an EnvirHero/Heroine Helper Activity"

"Dreaming of many costumes for the show"
1993 Magical Earth as a School Performance

Earlcourt School in Toronto, Earl Buxton school in Edmonton, and Indian Road Crescent, all put on plays of Magical Earth Secrets. The photo at the bottom is Kallie George who performed Eagle Child at a community fair, she is now a published author herself. At the top is St. Theresa's where the students helped me with the costumes for the New York show.

See "Magical Earth Costumes/Play"

"Saw a statue in a dream position"
1995 - Dale travels to Chitza Itza

Dale traveled to Chitza Itza, inspired by John Hugh Roberts in his Celtic writings who writes about travelling to Mexico. This was fascinating connection from one ancient culture to another. He was able to go to the inner pyramid and see a powerful sculpture.

Inside the inner pyramid at CHICHEN ITZA

The pyramid CHICHEN ITZA, Yucatan Mexico

See the "Travel Adventure" Activity

"You can manifest art to beauty"
1995 - Dodoland Online

Dodoland was launched online in 1995 as part of the Swiftsure Project & the goal was to teach artists, writers, art businesses, and book stores about the internet. It was the brainchild of David Godfrey. They chose the Dodoland story to launch the project and the first pages were posted online. Ivan Sinclair helped in the initial production. Josh Ardnt & Chris Martin took the design to the next level. It has had one million people visit it's Island of Eyes, Night Bubble, Giant Flower Island and Dragon Ship. After the first issue of the ezine Della & Dale took over production & created 600 free pages for teachers, parents and children in the world to experience their creativity and learn about the environment .

See "Make Story Map for Imaginary Place"

Della & Dale's
Third Eye Cycle 1996 - 2002

Third Eye Dream Cycle 1996-2002
"Third Eye" - egg tempera and acrylic washes 2013

In Cancer Recovery I am told "I have helped so many people in my life now it is time to help myself.". I am Divinely limited again but in my Dreams one August night in the Kootenay I find Visions A place called Third Eye where Sacred calls I visit August Moon - Buddha, Dalai Lama, & Moon Mother Where Druid Seers help you go on Quests to find Mermaids You find the Beauty Rose in the middle of a Tibetan Monks Circle Compassion Lotus Lakshmi and Muse Swan Saraswati witness And Faces morph, Buddha sits as Isis rythmically Ribbon dances I become a Bird and sprout huge wings to soar. I started Miracle Galaxy with eight Angels of Healing to guard me & others & heal.

"You can do art, dance & music to tell a story"
1997 - Start -up of Children's School in Gautelajara, Mexico

Della and Dale helped to start up of a Canadian school in Mexico. They both taught in the adult program. Della started for them a children program integating the arts to learn English. Dale & Laurie also helped start up this program. They are wearing storytelling hats for halloween day .The children were lively and they loved integrating the arts when learning English.

See the "Story Map for Imaginary Picture Book" Activity

"Stories come from many places."
1997 - Trips to Wales while living in England

Since we were living in England we went seven times to Wales. Dale was able to continue his research on the manuscipts. He went to various locations and we also went to Cornwall. Roberts has a story of him being saved as a child on a shipwreck off Cornwall and being adopted by Captain Roberts so we wanted to see Land's End.

Carn Fadryn, Lleyn, Gwynedd, a very special place.

The Rock formations at Lands End, Cornwall

"Create your own unique story"

1997- Della teaching in England- Dale multi-media"

I (Della) was teaching in England and did many storytellings of my stories including Dodoland and Magical Earth Secrets. In the last part of the trip we did a Dodoland workshop in Holland. The children created their own stories. We worked with Marijke Sluijer. Dale worked with a group in Birmingham who worked in multi-media. When we went back in 2004 we were able to use their media equipment.

See "Make a Bird Helmet"

"You are moving around the Medicine Wheel"
" In 1976 had a dream of of floating and landing in a prehistoric circle of stones. "

2000 - Visiting Stonehenge

When living in England we went to visit Stonehenge - The first time I went, it was the end of the day and I pleaded with them to let me see it. Fortunately, a private guide led me around and explained the different stones in the different directions, which were aligned with solstices and equinoxes. This influenced my Miracle Galaxy story. We were most interested in seeing Stonehenge as John Hugh wrote in his diaries about going there.

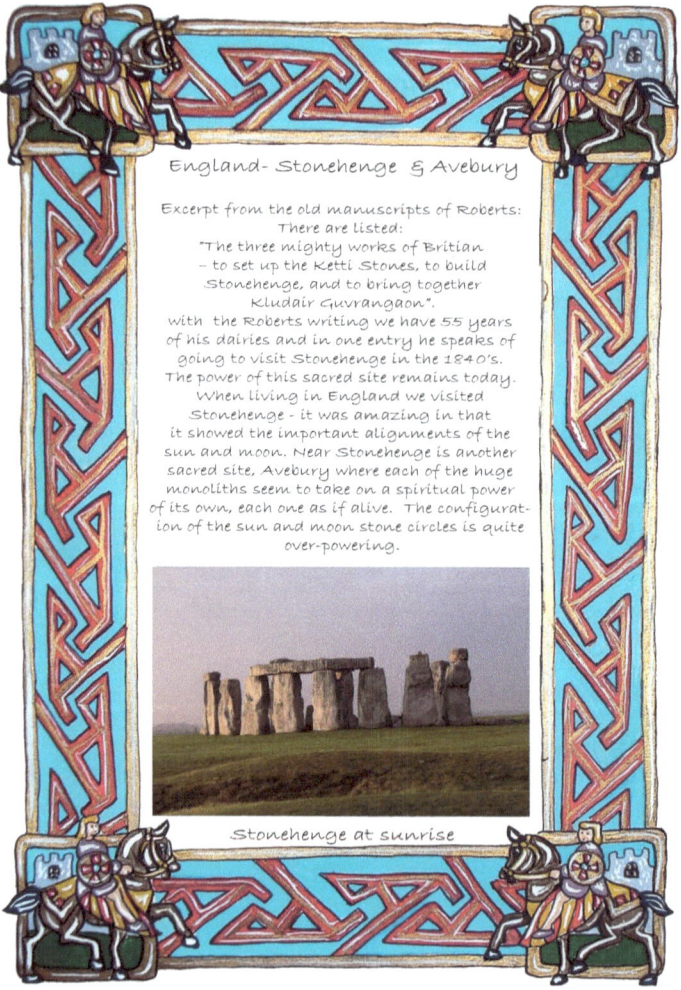

England- Stonehenge & Avebury

Excerpt from the old manuscripts of Roberts:
There are listed:
"The three mighty works of Britian - to set up the Ketti Stones, to build Stonehenge, and to bring together Kludair Guvrangaon".
with the Roberts writing we have 55 years of his dairies and in one entry he speaks of going to visit Stonehenge in the 1840's. The power of this sacred site remains today. When living in England we visited Stonehenge - it was amazing in that it showed the important alignments of the sun and moon. Near Stonehenge is another sacred site, Avebury where each of the huge monoliths seem to take on a spiritual power of its own, each one as if alive. The configuration of the sun and moon stone circles is quite over-powering.

Stonehenge at sunrise

See "Travel Adventure" Activity

"Use paintings as visions - as doorways"

2000 - August Full Moon Third Eye painting

The moon was full and in our house in the Kootenays, I (Della) had a mystical experience .. in the dream state between sleeping and awake I saw many spiritual goddesses and also Buddha and the Dalai Lama. I felt like my third eye had opened and this was allowing these visions. Many years later I did a painting representing this night. It was a time of expansion. A new doorway/portal had opened.

See "Create your own healing story" Activity

"saw a shaman with tattoos calling our names"

2001 - Dale & Della represent Canada at the World Island Festival - Jeju Island - Korea

Dale and I represented Canada at an Island Festival on Jeju Island, Korea, an island rich in natural beauty and traditional cultures. We arrived to take part in the 2nd WOFIC, 'World Festival for Island Cultures'. I storytold Magical Earth Secrets & Dale and I lead a workshop with nurses. Twenty seven Islands from many parts of the world came together to share their cultures and to build friendships across the oceans. To my surprise staying on the same floor in our hotel were people from Easter Island and Maori from New Zealand who had the same tattoos as I had in a deja-vu dream.

Sri Lanka

Adaman & Nicobar

Chile

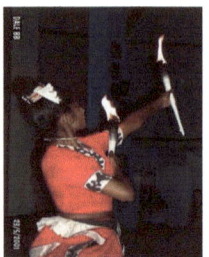
Sri Lanka

Cambodia

Chile

See the "Wind Dance" Activity

"Healing can happen in dreams" "The dream body can heal the physical body"

2001 - The Angels Come

In Cancer Recovery I was told by Dr. Rogers from the Inspire Health Center -"You have helped so many people in your life now it is time to help yourself" He encouraged me to write and paint a story. I proceeded to think of all the people supporting and helping me in real life and in dreams, and painted them as angels. The B.C. Cancer Agency had me write a short version of the story: The Willpower Angel came from realizing from Dr. Rogers, that my body had 3x the strength needed. The Kindness Angel grew out of compassion and was my sister Donna as she helped me with the drawings. The Peace Angel of an understanding that relaxation is essential to build the immune system. Intuition Angel from a nurse who told me to look inside myself to know.

Willpower Angel

Kindness Angel

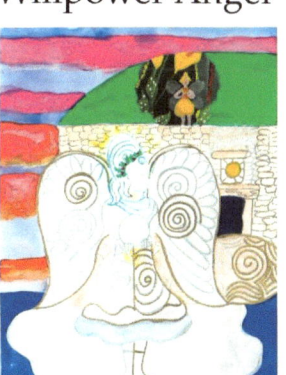
Intuition Angel

Peace Angel

See the "Create a Healing Story" Activity

"Shown the different spheres in the Miracle Galaxy as Mandalas."

2001-The Angels keep Coming!

When someone asked me: Where do the Angels come from in your story of the Miracle Galaxy? I answered some from dreams and some from thinking of family and friends. The Creativity Angel came from my creative mum. The Thank You Angel came when doing mediation at the end of a yoga session, when I was saying thanks for all the good things around me. Goodness Angel is from many friends who helped me to see the good side of life and the Dream Angel came in a dream and helps me visualize myself perfect, whole, and complete again. In the story, the Angels come and self healing becomes the miracle. Even today putting these Angels around me in visualization and meditation they feel like Guardians and feel good.

Creativity Angel

Thank you Angel

Goodness Angel

Dream Angel

See the "Create a Healing Story" Activity

" Please give us the wisdom of peace"

2001 - Peace Scroll created

Earth Wishes were collected during the years 1996 - 2001. One summer in travelling to Wales with the Earthchild Environment Foundation, we met the late Diana Rhodes in Machynlleth, Wales who was working in the country of green hills, turquoise rivers, myths and legends. Della originally heard about Diana's work and met her when Della was doing a workshop for educator's in Holland with Educare, coordinated by Marijke Sluitjer. Diana was creating a Peace Scroll which she has taken to the United Nations. It is in the form of a beautiful book called "Peace Scroll"- World Prayer for Peace and Healing- which was published in 2000 and 2001. The Children's Peace Section has been compiled by the Seed of Life Peace Foundation with the help of Earth Child Environment Foundation and Dodoland, collecting wishes. His holiness the Dalai Lama had honoured and given his blessings to this published Peace Scroll - (November 2001) by adding the Foreword. The Wishes, collected on-line and in workshops with Della and Dale, were sent to be added to the Scroll and also posted on the Dodoland in Cyberspace web-site. Here are a a few:

"My wish is that everyone should be treated the same and we could all get along in our world."
Kerry, Birmingham, England "I wish everyone will put litter in the bins and people say nice things to each other. Emma Strawford, Birmingham England. "I wish for everyone on the earth to be kind and helpful to each other." Beth, Birmingham, England "I wish that the world will be really bright."

See "The World we love" Activity

"Use your intuition to know the truth"

2001 Dale Teaching Speech Presentations

Dale spent seven years teaching Presentation Skills to international students in Vancouver at the V.E.C. His students were from all over the world - China, Korea, Japan, Russia, Thailand, South America, Mexico, Switzerland, and many other places in Europe. He was helping them get the ability to share their ideas. Many still keep in touch with him and tell him of their work they are doing and how they are.

"Travel anywhere, to another world, another planet or an imaginary world." - dream

2002 Travel Mural - Sundance Sounding Stones - Penn Kemp

I (Della) have been working on my book 'Miracle Galaxy' with the Angels of Healing. I worked on this while traveling around to various power spots connected to the ancient manuscripts Dale was researching. The students at Sun Dance created a large flower mural and each petal was a different student's travel story. We then had a workshop with author Penn Kemp, making sound for different stone circles. We had a show at the Community Art Gallery with my art & illuminations by Leo Del Pasqua, and photos by Dale of the Sacred Stones.

See the "Travel Adventure" Story Activity

Miracle Cycle - Kazuko

Kazuko did a Mandala workshop called Hamza Mandala in 2007. In 2009 she went to Ghana and made a Time Manadala. At the Kanazawabunko Festival the theme was the Earth's Future is the Children's Future. Each year at the Kazawabunko Festival there is a Parade of beautiful imaginative costume both children & adults have made. The Art School encourages the miraculous art creations of children. The Event Centre has many creative events for both children and adults. .

2007 Hamza El Din Days

Kazuko became friends with Hamza , (July 10, 1929 – May 22, 2006) who was a Nubian Egyptian/Sudanese composer, oud player, guitar player, and vocalist, and she organized musical events for him at her Centre and when he passed on Yokahama had a Memorial Concert honoring him.

2009 Ghana - Creating a Mandala with Kazuko

Kazuko made Time Mandalas in Ghana. In making Mandalas she explains " we are living in the different cultures in the same universe. We show three different times. 1st - the ancient history - how we got the earth around us and how ancient civilizations developed, 2nd- we think of when we were born and the history of our lives, and 3rd - today till the future. We can show cultures and through mandalas understand the world and how time changes things."

"See the Time Mandala Activity"

2009 African story – Coconut Elixir

This African story was performed which is a story about transformation.

2010 Asaba Art Square with Cafe Open

The Asaba Art Square opened to have an Event Centre and Cafe –They have events including all aspects of the arts – art, drama, music, dance, and all aspects of life including offerings by various hosts artistic meals.

2010 Asaba Art Square

The Asaba Art Square is a place to share our creativity. The community shares plays, songs, dance and art with each other.

Asaba Art Square Drum and Dance Event

There are many special events at the Asaba Art Centre. This one combined Dance and Drums.

Della & Dale's Miracle Cycle 2003 - 2009

Miracle Dream Cycle 2003- 2009

"Miracle" egg tempera and acrylic washes 2013

In your Dreams you find needed Miracles
A place of Self- Healing & a place to Spiritually Dance
You visit the Milky Way Galaxy
Where mandela spheres are revealed
You find Silver Feather energy & Healing Tools to Survive
Sitting by one you love on earth
And Communicating with family and friends
You help others by sharing visions, and helping them
Create their Healing Stories and Myths

"An eagle flew above viewing British Columbia"
Tomhu Huron Roberts - Early Canadian Artist

It was a miracle really that Dale received a collection of paintings from his mother who inherited them in 1979 from Charles Steele (the first boy registered to be born in Vancouver in 1886). He was the grandson of John Hugh Roberts, a Welsh mystic, whose writings Dale has pursued and published into 6 books. Dale produced shows of the art collection across Canada, starting in Vancouver, to Edmonton and then on to Toronto.

The view north from Quebec and 10th Ave Vancouver

Rail Crew near Lillooet, BC 1884-5

"I saw giant praying hands coming out of a lake."

2003 - SouthCoast Plaza, Newport Beach, California, Storytelling at the Festival of Children

I told the Dodoland story on the Jewel Court stage at the Festival for Children at Newport Beach, California. There was 50 charities who all helped children with displays. We put up links to all of their webpages in Dodoland online. My storytelling was dedicated to two men who lived in California, the late Dr. Dick Mazurek who published Dodoland, and to the artist, the late Doug Riseborough. who believed in my work.

See the "Make an Angel" Activity

"You are a mermaid"
2004 - Mermaid Synchronicity

I had a powerful dream of a mermaid statue at a town square. I was to take a bus there but had little money. In Robert's Druid manuscipts that Dale was researching, grandmother and friends were called mermaids. I woke up knowing Dale and I should go to Cornwall to some of the Stone Circles. We stayed at Sue Bladdon's home and we were shown around Cornwall by a very intuitive woman, Barbera Tremain, who could tell by holding the ancient manuscripts where we should go. The first place she took us to was a church in Zennor which had a story of a Mermaid attached to it and a special Mermaid bench was in the church. She also took us to Stone Circles and a Mermaid Cove.

Mermaid chair in Zennor Mermaids by Della Burford

See "Create a Healing Story" Activity

"In a dream was told the Druids are coming"

2004 Sacred Place Visiting Power Spots

Dale and I went to many Sacred Sites connected to the research on the mystical writings of John Hugh Roberts. These are outlined in Dale's Druidical Quest We went across from Barsley Island (Teman). and also to Stonehenge, Avebury, Bocsacwen Un, many Stone Circles in Cornwall and to New Grange in Ireland. Photos below are Avebury.

Some of the wonderful stones at Avebury

See the "Travel Adventure" Activity

"Put rose petals under your pillow"
2004 - Create you own Healing Story Holland

In seeing my Angels of Healing from Miracle Galaxy, the students created their own personal Angels that helped them when in a crisis and wrote a healing story. Dale shared a Medicine Wheel storytelling of his Druidical Quest.

See "Create your own Healing Story" Activity

"Angels will speak to you" "Shown in a dream how the Miracle Galaxy looked"

2005 - Miracle Galaxy Dream

In a dream of clarity in 2005 I was shown, in a lucid dream a milky way-like galaxy where the eight angels lived. When I woke up I had to paint this immediately and could not stop until I finished.

This became the Miracle Galaxy. It looked so Milky Way like, and I was surprised at a health conference a few weeks later, the man speaking from a herbal company started talking about the signifigance of the milky way to the Mayan people. I went up to him and thanked him. He went on to tell me of a woman he knew who communicated with angels who phoned him. He was climbing Chitza Itza at the time and she told him she had been told by Archangel Michael that at the next event he was at to talk about signifigance of the milky way to the Mayan people. He then proceeded to tell me this must have happened for me to know about it. Synchronicty at play again.

See the "Create a Healing Story" Activity

"You can visit a wise one in your dream"
2005 - Create Your Own Myth Class

I (Della) created a storytelling, writing and art program in Vancouver. Students were creating and telling many different kinds of stories - Myths, Fables, Stories with Emotion and Drama, and some with Travel. They even are creating their own original Hero/Heroines and Imaginary Maps. The students were inspired by my stories and art. They also combined a short animation and soundloops to share their "Imaginative Mythic Stories" online.
Dale taught Public Speaking and Business Language at a nearby school.

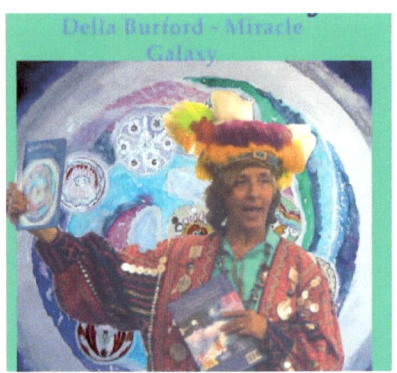

See the "Create a myth" Activity

You need a special energy to create illuminations"

2008 - Sharing Vision - Dale's Travels published and Illuminated Books

Dale produced Druidical Quest in 2008 after many years of travels to research the old manuscripts that he was given by his mother, written by John Hugh Roberts. He had had four manuscripts beautifully illuminated by Leo del Pasqua for books published in 2014 to appeal to all ages, After years of research it was good to share this vision.

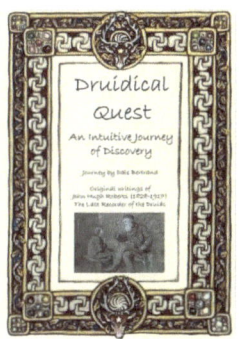
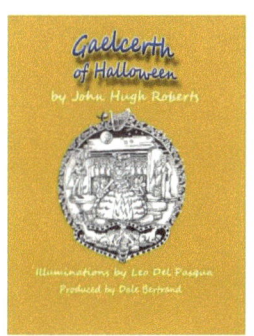

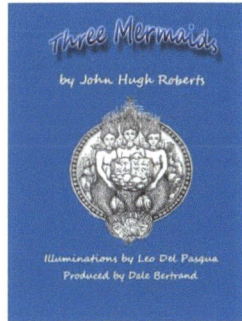

See "Travel Adventure" Stories

"all the different colored children have light"
2008 Storytelling in Mexico Los Ayala & Gaudalajara

It was a hot day in Mexico in a little fishing village when I (Della Burford) was storytelling Dodoland Adventures and Miracle Galaxy. The kids and teacher were awesome. I went afterwards through a sacred stone site with Dale Bertrand. Though we were leaving the next day, felt I must go to Mexicaltitlan. Took a bus to San Blas and as synchronicity has it, I met Renee Watson in the square in San Blas and though I was a stranger to her she said she would drive me to Mexicaltitlan. We are still friends today.

See " Make a travel story" card

"you can dream about sacred spots"

2009 Visiting Foco Tonal with Dance Teacher Gloria Arroyo

The first photo is my Dance mentor Gloria and on the right of her my Dance teacher Roberto who was teaching me Mexican dance. The second is her dancing. Gloria Arroyo took me to a special place called Foco Tonal where Don Jose Sebastian Zamora astrally travelled and discovered a power spot when doing a healing. He built a series of pillars in the location. When you stood in the middle your voice echoed. I had dreamt of the small figures and the castle at the entrance before going there. It was deja-vu for me to go there.

Inside like a deja-vu dream miniature toy story settings

A fairy-like castle/church

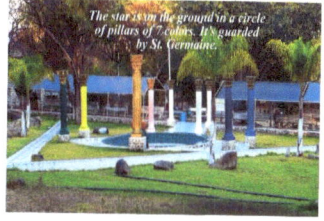
The star is on the ground in a circle of pillars of 7 colors. It's guarded by St. Germaine.

See "Wind Dance" Activity

"I and the earth are one - I love the earth"

2009 - Eco Project in Korea

I (Della) went twice to Korea to lead workshops for children. One was at Kyeogju (2007) and the other at Gapyeong. The children learned creativity with Dodoland, and the environment with the Magical Earth Secrets. I also shared Miracle Galaxy and they imagined angels who helped them. I worked with Bo Young to make picture books, with a group of 25 children. Also worked with Jacquie Howardson on environmental themed projects.

See " Story Map for an Environmental Story"- Short but Good Story and Illustrations. "

"saw a beaded Medicine Wheel"
2008 - Dale in Haida Gwaii

Dale did a project for B.C. Aboriginal Tourism in Event Management in Haida Gwaii. He was thrilled to be in this beautiful part of British Columbia and the people who lived there.

See "Four winds - Four directions Medicine Wheel Activity

Della & Dale's
Divine Cycle 2010-2018

"Shaman's Eye" watercolor & acrylic 2011

In your Dreams you find the Divine
A place where the Human and Divine co-create
Where Eagle, White Tiger, & Deer Dance
You visit Dream Shaman, Blue Buddha, & Druid Wizard
Where there is Validification of dreams value
You continue to Honor your dreams
And help others to Honor theirs
Reminded that Dreams are Wise and very Precious
In your Dreams you Can and Do Change World Essence

"I walked thru the Medicine Wheel to the edge, looked at myself and out to the cosmos"
"Meditated on Mount Kailash and felt like I went there in my dream."

2011 - Painted Spirit Stories book by Aaron Zerah

Aaron Zerah asked if I could paint his book of three Spiritual stories. I would read the stories and then dream on them. I would get many ideas from my dreams. Aaron was always amazed that I was able to do this. One story had Mount Kailash in it and I meditated on it and dreamt of it before painting. The stories are now being shared with many children all over the world 6000 of these book have been given as gifts and viewed or downloads on freekidsbook.org. This makes us happy as they are folktales for everyone.

See "The World We Love" Activity

"Dream of the dakini stamping the ground"

2011 - Dream of Dream Goddess

When I was first learning the mische technique and studying with Oleg Korolec, I had a dream of a dakini stamping the ground. She was saying, "It was to get rid of the greed and she said her stamping the ground would make the earth tremor, to wake people up. The message was for all of the world. This was just weeks before the Big earthquake . When I woke up I thought since the figure was blue, that it was the Shiva, but later in studying Dream Yoga realized it was Salgye Du Dalma, the dakini who represents clarity and luminosity, in Bon Tibetan Buddhism. I did a painting and included her in it with Buddha & Sacred Elephants. This painting was shown at the School of Fine Art in Peru in 2016.

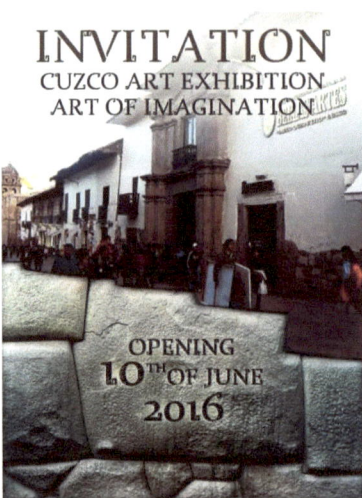

See the "Inner Dream Mandala" Activity

"Saw a First Nations man who with a clap of thunder gave me beadwork"

2011 - Make an Angel for Japan - Della's Workshop in Toronto

In hearing of the devastation in Japan with the tsunami and earthquake, I (Della) wondered like so many others what could be done? She was happy to be asked by Joy Kogawa to be part of the support team on the Toronto to Japan initiative to show solidarity and support for Japan. In knowing the Toronto to Japan project was sending videos to Japan, she thought of an idea to do a workshop with the "Miracle Galaxy" story and combine art and good wishes for the people of Japan. David Walsh at 6 St. Joseph Place encouraged her to do the workshop in downtown Toronto in the heart of the city. Make an Angel for Japan was about creating positive energy.

In the middle of the back is second from the left Alice Brownlee, Howard Jerome and Pat Brennan, On the left is Yasmin Glanville, Della & friend.

"be what you want to be"
you can fly in your imagination"

2011 - Impov of Dodoland with Paripurna Dance School

The children did an improv performance of my story of "Journey to Dodoland" but we called it "Dodoland - On the Way to Bali" it was really fun for everyone. We had a Dancing Flamingo, Bird Dance, Banana Body Band the Eagle Child, and Elemental Dodo in the play. of my storycalled "Magical Earth Secrets". I Made and his son made the Eagle Child puppet come alive.

This is I Made Sijia, I Made Sidia, Sugi, Suastini and Della

See "Story Map of an Imaginary Picture Book"

"Quest are sometimes meant to be done alone"
2012 - Studied Painting in Vienna Went to the Klagenfurt Chapel

Della (I) had dream with Ernst Fuchs and decided to study painting at the Old Masters/New Visions with Philip Rubinov Jacobson. Another dream was to see Ernst Fuchs Chapel, in Klagenfurt. Many people said they wanted to go but couldn't, but as it is with vision quests I was meant to go alone. And as often on a quest, there was many obstacles and there was on this one, but the end result was I saw a precious jewel.

Learning the mische technique with Philip Rubinov Jacobsen

At the Fuchs chapel in Klagenfurt

See "Travel Adventure" Activity

"We come together to dream"

2012 Storytelling Austria - Arthoff

While in Austria, I (Della) storytold various stories for a video at the Arthhoff Gallery near Vienna. The group studying painting with Philip Rubinov Jascobsen also had an art show in the Arthoff Gallery. I sold a print of my painting "Transformation".
There was another show in Vienna and I (Della) met many artists who she included in "We come together to dream" in her Dream Wheels book.

See the " Inner Dream Mandala" card

"We can transform in dreams"
2012 - Workshop Spirit of Writing & Art Balipurnati

Norah Burford and I coordinated an event at Balipurnati. Philip Rubinov Jacobsen led the Painting workshop. Other artists from Europe came - De Es, Wolfgang, Peter & Vesna and Mantra assisted Phil. I taught inspiration and storytold at I Made Sidia's Dance School. Many talented artists came to add to the energy - Sal, Dale, Sylke, Aubrey, Lana, Irene, Michelle to name a few. The theme was transformation and how we can shift energy. I (Della) led an Ïnspiration" workshop with my books.

See the "Cosmic One" Activity

"Look into your dreams, and you will find out more about who you are."

2012 - We come together to dream

While studying in Vienna, I was working on my Dream Wheels book. Decided from guidance in a dream to ask artists if they had any paintings which came from dreams. Put them together with a poem in the book "We come together to dream".

Thanks to (L to R) Daniel Mirante, Philip Rubinov Jacobsen, Kuba Ambrose, Vesna Krasnec, De Es ,Peter Gric, Liba W.S. Cynthia Re Robbins, Irene Vincent, Andrew Gonzalex, Mark Lee, Rolland Proulx, Gabriela Garza Padilla, Aloria Weaver, David Heskin & Jennifer McCluen.

See Inner Dream Wheels Activity

Divine Cycle - Kazuko & Ruu*Ruu

2011 there was a meeting after the Big Earthquake in Japan of people concerned on what to do. Kazuko told "The Magical Earth Secrets" story and Ruu*Ruu said she wanted to do a play of it. She was perfect as she makes such magical costumes. She was told in a dream to make God Ornaments and some are very ethereal. The story has been performed many times since 2012 - two being at Kazawabunko Festival and at Earth Day in Tokyo.
In 2015 Kazuko & Ruu*Ruu travelled to Mexico to meet Della & Dale and discussed future plans. Kazuko also travelled to Bhutan, Laos & Minnesota and worked with the children in making Time mandalas. The 50th Anniversary of Kazuko Art School was in 2018 and many people celebrated her success. Dale and Della went to Japan to join the Celebrations.

Ruu* Ruu's Celestial Atelier

Ruu*Ruu who has been making hats for 30 years had a dream. She saw hats that she called "god-hats" made by celestial angels. The hats were crowns which represented people who live a life like an angel, goddess or champion. She was perfect to meet Kazuko and start the designs for Majical Rainbow.

2013 Kanazawabunko Festival

At the Festival the performers dance "Majical Rainbow. Below is a tipi in the Indigenours Plaza. Kazuko created this as part of the Festival as she feels the spiritual ways, love of nature and peace of the Indigenous people is important.

Majical Rainbow at the Kanazawabunko Festival 2013

Story/Painting by Author Della Burford from Canada
Magical Earth Secrets published by the Western Canada
Wilderness Commitee Production & Costumes - Ruu*Ruu

  Thanks to Kazuko Asaba. for sharing the book with Ruu*Ruu Performers: Hiromi Inti Uezumi, Meena Surya Sangita, Ricky Risa Nishizawa, Takuma Hara, Uoomin Asami, Hoashi Hirosuke, Yuhki Oomoto, Ishio Yuki, Yasuhiro Zum Takeda, Kohei Fujiwara, Atsuko Suga, and Momo Nakagawa. Uusuhiro Zun, Koehl Mujwara, & others.

2013 Majical Rainbow- Tokyo

Majical Rainbow" from Della's book being performed in Tokyo
photo by Masanao Showjit Sugyama

Production / Costumes Ruu*Ruu Spearheaded also by Kazuko Asaba, Little Eagle Child- Kazumi Oomoto, Eagle Child - Yasuhiro Zum Takeda, Mother Earth - Tara Kashahara, Earth Seed --Ricky Rusi Nishizawa, Sweetwater - Yukhi Oomoto, Satri Abe, Sunbeam - Uoomin Asami, Sun Ray - Kazyuki Mitani, Starlight - Hiromi Inti Uezumi, Lovewind - Momo Nakagawa, Starbird- Ishio Yuki, Crystal Wish - Aki Noguchi ,
There were many wonderful musicians at the shows in Japan as well to name a few Chie Narita, Ricca Rogues Kanemura, Ale, Ishio Uke, Takuya Lida, Kys Kono, Tak Suetomi, Makoto Takahashi, Bun Kilimba and Kia Isechi . Thanks also to Koseki Yuji, Hiroko Ishizuka, Hoashi Hirosuke, Takuma Hara, ShoTanishi, Nishi Tanishi, Naoyuki Nande, Ricca Kaemuara, Yoko Izuhara, Tomomi Hasegawa , Takumaa Har, Tutoma Mutaguti, Hitomi Inti Uezumi, Nao Yak Nade, Aike Oukibo, Tutonic Mutaguti , Koshi Yugim Aike, Oukibo, Yamaguchi Ai,Yucco, & Maulani Laamb, Meena Surya Anjita, Fiori Hanawo, Makoko Tsujimura, Seung Yong Kim. - .thanks for the video.

"Many costumes came in dreams"
2013 Magical Earth Secrets - Majical Rainbow - Japan

So many people have have come together to share the story of our love for the earth and wanting to protect it. One secret in the story is : Ï and the Earth are One ", I love the Earth and will take care of the Earth".

Photo by Masanao Showjit Sugyama

See Magical Earth Costume/Play Activity/

"Praying hands come out of the ocean to help"
Newtown Peace Park Handbook
"together we create a culture of kindness"

I was thrilled to be included in this free handbook
with many authors that was produced to help
the people of New town to help bring peace.
It was produced and edited by Julie Lyonn Lieberman.
It includes two of my Angels from Miracle Galaxy.
It also includes Chapter topics: Forgiveness
I am a Peacemaker, Miracle Galaxy, Return to Creation,
Helping Your Child Cope In Times of Terror,
A Community of Creators, ... The Raven's Story ...
The Artist and the Holocaust ...

Authors:
Azim Khamisa   Douglas Noll
Della Burford   Manitonquat
Robert Zucker   Si Lewen
Robert Fritz   Aaron Zerah

Edited by Julie Lyonn Lieberman

See "Create a Healing Story" Activity.

"You will jump in a lotus flower"
2013 Journey to the Lotus published -"All is one"

Journey to the Lotus was written and painted in India in 1973. I traveled to India in the 70's resulted in many revelations, inspirations, poems and paintings. Transformation, universal love, and knowledge of the chakras were seeds that were planted that became foundation stones and it resulted in shaping my future paintings and stories. My trip to India influenced my work with Humanity, Mother Earth & Spirit over the years. Before publishing this as a book many years later, I had a dream of many Spiritual Ones astrally travelling with their auras merging. The Mother of the World protected them.

See the "Cosmic One" Activity

"Saw a Dream Wheel and pictures of events from the Wheels around." "If dreams are manifested .. you dream stronger."

2014 - Collaborative Show with Karja - Dream Wheels

Della and Karja had a collaborative show in Bali with his Colorful inspired art and her paintings from the Dream Wheels book. Della led a workshop and spoke on how she has created the Dream Wheels book. She had many dreams to help her in the design of the book. For 40 years she made a Mandala each year and this helped her manifest many dreams as writing, art & plays. Her dreams are for self growth and also many for humankind.

Della with her Dream Wheel from 2013 - Photo Fabrizio Bellardarti taken at Spirit of Writing & Art

See "Make a Dream Wheel" Activity and "Inner Dream Wheel"

"had a dream of a ferris wheel with art"
2014 Spirit of Writing and Art in Bali .. "Bali feeds the Soul"

Norah and I organized, and Dale helped host, a workshop to increase creativity, opening chakras, sharing dream wheels, new visions, and imagination. Wayan Karja's space was the studio and we had a collaborative show of his work and the Dream Wheels paintings. We held the sacred space with acu- yoga, painting, and included Made Sida's family, & Charlyne Chiasson's Elemental Feng Shiu energy (she started on her book in 2011 - completed in 2018), Irene's painting & Dale's workshop - Medicine Wheels & photos. Fabrizio Belardetti's photos from "Bali feeds our Souls".

Held space together : Dale, Made Sidia, Irene, Charlyne

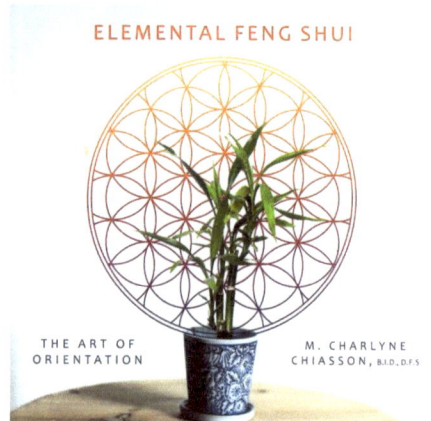

Charlyne's book 2018 Elemental Feng Shui

Della and Karja had a collaborative show "Dream Wheels"
See "Make a Inner Dream Mandala"

"Make a wish for the earth"
2014 -Earth Day Parade
100% Parade Ruu Ruu

For many years Ruu* Ruu has participated with 100 % Parade in Parades to express Creativity, Love and Peace. There are many beautiful people parading. They are different artists and creative people who are part of the community.

See "Color and Sound" Activity

"What do you see in the wing of a bird"
2014 - Show in Ottawa & Montreal

Della showed her art in Montreal and in Ottawa with the Society for Art of Imagination. . She was able to share the painting "Third Eye" which showed a mystical experience she had in 2001. She was glad to have a chance to meet Brigid Marlin, who started the group decades ago and has devoted her life to teaching artists the old master techniques of mische painting and organizing shows & sharing visio**ns.**

See "Inner Dream Mandala" Activity

"Everyone has a unique horse of their own"
2014 - Dream Class - Robert Moss

In 2014 met Robert Moss, dream teacher who was teaching a class in Vancouver, and enjoyed the dream exploration. Ended up studying almost a year and getting to be friends with many fellow dream adventurers. We went deeper into the dream world together. In one class we went to the Cinema of Lost Dreams, and I found a story I worked on years ago with my mother (1980's) and was told to revive it as it was important for the world. The story is about losing dream and finding them again, so the synchronicity with the topic of the class was there. Just last week when in a class and asked to go to the future, saw this story again and I was riding my Spirit Horse which is the essence of oneself.

See"Make an Inner Dream Mandala" Activity

Meeting Paul Hogan - Toronto Sri Lanka, Cambodia

Heard about Paul many years ago in Toronto & just yesterday again. Feel his work is so relevent to today, so want to share a little about him:

This is where it started..Imagine a Butterfly Peace Garden. Paul Hogan is an artist from Canada who has worked for forty years with image, story, myth and theatre in creative collaboration with forgotten and marginalized people at home and abroad. Starting with apparitional street theatre in Toronto in the early 70's he helped develop gardens of healing for physically challenged children in Canada and for youth affected by war, natural disaster and genocide in Sri Lanka and Cambodia. He now works with the Garden Path "Project Phoenix" in Sri Lanka and with local artists in Toronto adapting his Out-of-the-Box Curriculum to contemporary North American conditions. Paul originated, designed and developed the Garden Path Out-of-the-Box Curriculum, a set of handmade interactive toys which encourage cooperation and cultivate community through the practice and cultivation of the arts have been developed and are now being field tested and implemented. See his work and book "Beautiful Nonsense"

See www.thegardenpath.ca/

2015 - Kazuko & Ruu Ruu visit Mexico to meet Della & Dale

Kazuko, Ruu*Ruu, Della and Dale meet in Mexico to discuss future plans. We met in Puerto Vallarta and the visited the little fishing village of Los Ayala. Kazuko invited us to come in 2018 to the 50th Anniversary Celebration of her Art School in Japan.

"Saw a group of people dancing in a circle"

Storytelling with I Made Sidia

I and I Made Sidia have collaborated on many projects with storytelling, combining story with art, and story with dance with his students from the Paripurna Dance School. In 2017 he shared his life size puppet show that he was taking to a conference in India. I gifted the Rainbow Wings puppet to his family.

"On Robert Moss's Soul Map you find the country closest to your soul ... for me this is Bali"

More Art and Story in Bali

Thanks to my sister Norah who has organized our Spirit of Writing and Art Workshops in Bali. After the workshop I often went to storytell at Pelangi School with the children. I shared "Bali feeds the Soul" & dream books.

Bali feeds your Soul - with photo by Fabrizio Bellardetti & Dale .. L - Della & sister Norah R- Pelangi School

"find your spirit guides in your dreams
2016 - Spirit of Writing & Art

The people attending our retreats have made the retreats so special.. to dream together makes a tight freindship.

Wallace, Grace, Fran, Susan, Dale, Della, Charlyne, Irene, Norah and Fabrizio who took the photo.

2016 - Wallace, Sylke, Sahara Nez, Freeman, Leema, Charlyne Della, Eric, Norah, Ayden, Holly, Grace & Dale & friends.

"See the Ïnner Dream Mandala" Activity

"I saw a pink & blue angel in my dream"

"Saw a crystalline fairy in my dream"

2016 Nanaimo Art Gallery

Dale and I were part of the Nanaimo Art Gallery residencey program that visited schools. I did many Angel projects and Dale Enviro-Posters.

"Body Energy Rainbows" Activity

"Dance to tell your story to the world"
2011-2018 Collaboration with I Made Sidia - Paripurna Dance Company

Each of the eight years we have gone to Bali, we have been able to do something special with I Made Sidia and his family, Wayan Suastini, Sugi and and Arix . We have done improvs of my stories, storytellings, and art. They presented dances, masks, & puppet shows and taken us to performances of Bali Agung (with 150 performeres) at the Bali Safari and also Desa Visesa in Ubud (a beautiful retreat space with restaurants) where we saw a spectacular outdoor show.

Suastini, Della & Made Sidia

Bali Agung

Performance of the Rice Goddess at Desa Visesa - Ubud 2018

See the "Make an Environmental Play" Card

"Inner and Outer Space are equally important."

2016 - Visionary Alchemy One Space - New York

It meant a lot ot me to share with other artists at this show which featured Society for Art of Imagination artists. Visionary art shows inner worlds, and I feel this is so important today in our technically inclined world. There are so many inner realms to explore and the artists showed some of these in this show. Since I went to Interor Design School in New York in 1965, and to the World Fair where Outer Space was emphasized, as it was the time of the first exploration on the moon, I found it fascinating that fifty years later the exhibition I was participating in was "Visionary Alchemy & it was about exploring inner space.

See "Create an Inner Dream Mandala"

" I will love, and take care of the earth"
2016 - Performance - Tokyo Majical Rainbow

In 2016 a show of the Magical Earth Secrets by Della Burford) is made into a beautiful show called "Majical Rainbow". This was in Tokyo. It was spearheaded by Kazuko and Ruu Ruu, who is also the costume designer. There are many imaginative dancers, actors and musicians involved. It's theme is to love and protect the earth.

See "Environmental Hero/Heroine Costumes"

"Parade to share our unique selves"
2016 - Kunitachi Parade 100% Parade Tokyo

Each year a Parade is organized in Tokyo. This year the theme was creativity. Models modelled clothes in the parade costumes that Rock star Kiyoshiro Imawanu wore. Ruu*Ruu was designing clothes for him. Many people had their own creative costumes. Below are the performers of Majical Rainbow which was at the culmination of the Parade.

See the "Magical Earth Play" Activity

2016 Contemporary Dance Festival Kazuko in Palestine

Kazuko participated in doing art backgrounds (stage art) for a dance performances with a Peace theme in Palestine. This was at the Ramallah Dance Co. Yoshiko Chuma also does various projects with the Dance Company. She has asked Kazuko to collaborate on various Peace themed projects. Yoshiko, who lives in New York, is a dancer, a choreographer and the director of the Bessie Award winning performance art group The School of Hard Knocks.

2017- Kazuko visits Laos

Kazuko went to Laos to make Time Mandalas with the children. They were Mon which is a Mountain Tribe. The children were used to doing needlework and small stitches so made very fine detail. Everything was done very sensitively.

2016- Kazuko visits Bhutan

Time Mandalas were made with Kazuko in Bhutan, the country where happiness is a priority. Kazuko found the children to be very peaceful, quiet and calm. She felt it was a very stable culture.

"Artist are sitting together on the Medicine Wheel"
2017 - Spirit of Writing and Art - Society for Art of Imagination

Workshop & Show featuring the art of the Society for Art of Imagination and Balinese artists - Wayan Karja, Gusti Lanang, Made Sure , Aboetd Art & friend. Also in the photo is Sylke Gande (sacred art), Melissa Marineau & Dale. I (Della) workshopped Ocean Painting, and Dream work. Dale facilitated Medicine Wheels and Irene Vincent - the mische technique.

Irene demonstrating to Melissa & Yanksi Sova
See the "Ocean Painting" Activity Card

"When studying with Michael Reed Gach had a dream of an Energy Fire Wizard - made a drawing showing the extraordinary channels Michael taught and how energy flowed in the body." Dreaming also of "dancing in a hexagram"

Studying Acu - Yoga & Acupressure

I loved Michael Reed Gach's book Acu-yoga and included it as part of my yoga practice. It combines acupressure pionts & yoga. I was introduced to it when Dodoland was being preformed at Ananda Ashram in the 1985. In 2015 decided to learn more about Acupressure and took two courses with Michael - one - Self Healing & a certificate course for practising. Since travelling to Japan & my story being performed in Japan found it fascinating that Michael was trained in Zen Shiatsu from Japanese Zen Priest Reuho Yamada who learned from Master Shizuto Masanaga. Michael is Founder and Director of the Acupressure Institute in Berkeley. Since studying I have included Acu-Yoga in classes in Bali. Below is a photo of Michael and also a quick rough sketch upon awakening done after my dream - Energy Fire Wizard that came from being inspired from studying the extraordinary channels in his class.

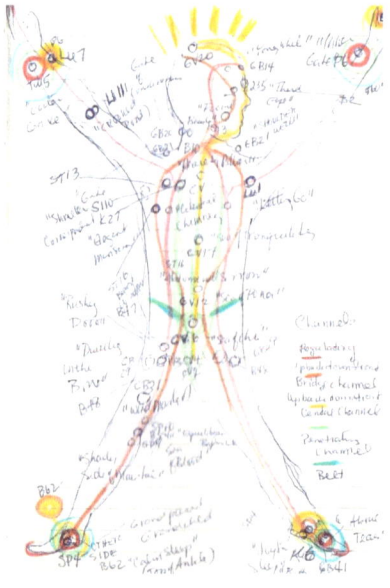

"Dream of people sitting around a crystal... when "om" was sounded the crystal lit up"
"There was a ring of light and many spiritual leaders inside - one was Yogi Bhajan, another Tenzin Wangyal Rinpoche"

Studied Dream Yoga with Tenzin Wangyal Rinpoche

My sister Norah gave me the book "The Tibetan Yogas of Dream and Sleep" in 2008. I loved that it was a Ancient technique that included Dreaming and Yoga. I was inspired by it and finally got to study with Tenzin in 2017. The approach became clearer and now use it daily. I love that it includes dreaming from the chakras as I have included how important the chakras are in many of my painting and stories. I am in gratitude.

"Many artists will sit on the Medicine Wheel"
2017- Imagination Reigns Show

I (Della) organized a show of the "Society for Art of Imagination" to share their work with Bali

"Imagination Reigns" in Ubud Bali
at Spirit of Writing and Art - Jan 27th - Feb 5th 2017 Opening 27th 4-8
Hosted by Della Burford/Norah Burford & Dale Bertrand
Show of the Members of the "Society for Art of Imagination"

Brigid Marlin-Founder   Della Burford-Coord   Jean Pronovost   France Garrido

Wayan Karja Host in Bali   Benny Anderson   Cynthia Re Robbins   Debra Keirce   Gaia Orion   Kathleen Scarboro

Olga Spiegel   Miguel Tio   Michael Coleman   William Otto   Irene Vincent   Liba W.S.

Lyne Lafontaine   Joanne St. Cyr   Rosemary Stehlik   Chris Dyer   Margot Bussiere   Heiidi Taillefer   Jerome Bertrand (former admid)

Georgina Smith   Dustyn Lucas   Ricky Schaede   Zeerka   Andrew Gonzalez   Fay Marineau   Sylke Gande

"honor your dreams by manifesting them"

2017 - Performance - Majical Rainbow

Lively 100% Parade group in costumes for the Majical Rainbow - adaption from the book Magical Earth Secrets. by Della Burford, Costumes by Ruu*Ruu.

Many people involved .. just listing a few :
Rainbow wings- Momoka , Wise Lotus One : Kazuko Asaba, disciples: Hyogo (rice balls), Atsuko Hirose - spring: Yu - summer, Miki , winter-Masa, Earth Child - Ricky Risa Nishizawa, SunRay- Ugami Satoru Ugajin , Flower Spirit: Yuzo (Omusubi)
Sacred Water: Satori, Satri Abe, Ai Also Ai no Kaze .. Aimi Ennigrou
Bird of Yukari star: Yumi Shimizu Tomomi Shimizu Ami
Crystal Wish - Yuko Nawa Inui
Archangel Color helper: Meena Surya Sangita
Music: Hana Wo Flower Spirit Tomoo Nakashima
Conch blower Hyougo Nakashima

See "Make a Magical Earth Costume/Play

2017-Kazuko in Minnesota Pueblos - Sun Dance Mandala

In Minnesota Kazuko went and made a Mandala around the Sundance Ceremony with children and adults. Some of the children were the grandchildren of Dennis Banks.

2017 Memorial for Dennis Banks

Kazuko held a memorial for Dennis Banks, co-founder of the American Indian movement, who had toured Japan previously giving a message of hope for the future and was for those who needed ceremony and to smell the sweetgrass & sage and accept its deep meaning for a good life.

This is a photo from 2016 of Dennis on the left, in the middle Enshou Yamada, and on the right the Ainu elder Haruzo Urakawa.

*"I saw gloves of different colors that
were for travelling to different places"*

"Be Well Princess" Story for Adaea

I have included the 'Be Well Princess' story, in the front of our Divine Section, as a Memorial for Adaea. Adaea is one of 3 people in the Spirit World who the book 'Art for One World' is dedicated to. Being the granddaughter of our best friends, she loved princesses so the Princess story was written for her. She fought hard and we saw her grow to be the Angel Princess This story is written in memory of Adaea who spent her last months at the B.C. Children's Hospital. She was an angel is this life and will be in our memories forever and help us all find our inner Prince and Princesses.
These photos below are from 'Camp Good time', summer fun for those who have fought cancer and their families.
This story, in her memory, is for all, who are in anyway are in need of the gift to "Be Well" again - including all ages. The last photo is her cousins and Fairy Princess friends who came to celebrate her 6th birthday. Much love to all - Della and Dale

See the "Nature Prince/Princess" Activity

"Had a dream of a group of Fairy Princesses sitting by a bed for comfort, coloring, and sharing food - they had butterfly wings! "

 2018 - Be Well Fairy Princess Story

Once upon a time, there was a little girl called Adaea who lived in a castle with her family and who loved to dance and paint. She had been given the gift of a pair of dancing shoes and paint brushes by her two grandmothers. But then something unexpected happened. The Princess became very sick and had to go to the hospital. She worked hard, and all those around her too, at her getting stronger.

The King and Queen of the land proclaimed that she be visited by eight Prince and Fairy Princesses (beautiful in the inside) from different parts in the land. The first to come was the Red Willpower Fairy Princess who brought her a pair of 'Be Well Running Shoes' and said to her, "use your willpower to become stronger and better and you will be able to run a little bit further every day". A whole group of running soul friends got together to run and show their support for her. It helped her to know others were supporting and thinking of her. Her favorite animal was her dog Calla.

The second to come was the Orange Dream Fairy Princess who gave her a 'Be Well Mirror'. She had to look at it and visualize herself well and healthy again. She said, "I am perfect, whole and complete." At first, this was hard but then she eventually saw herself radiant. The princesses favorite animal was the elephant.

Third came the Yellow Thank You, Prince, who brought a 'Be Well Thank You' gift of a basket of fruit. Each fruit she ate she was to say something she was thankful for in the world. This basket of fruit was magical and each time it became empty it filled up again with beautiful fruit. His favorite animal was the cat.

Be Well Fairy Princess Story

The fourth to come was the Green Goodness Fairy Princess who had a gift of a 'Heart Cushion'. She was told to think of good thoughts, and each time she did, she heard her heartbeat. As she surrounded herself with her family and friends they also gave good thoughts and her heart throbbed. They loved her so much they made Block Sign saying Love. Princess's favorite animal was the Baby Panda who gave Adaea kisses and hugs.

And then fifth Blue Prince and his Dolphin who represented strength came along. He had the 'Be Well Ball'. He told her to visualize herself throwing the sickness away as she got the balls higher and higher. As Adaea used her strength the ball went higher.

The Indigo Good Wishes Fairy Princess came sixth and gave her a 'Be Well Bell' and said to make wishes, Loving thoughts and strong prayers and the bell would ring. Her friend was a hummingbird and as it rang she heard, Om So Hum.

The seventh was the Purple Imagination Fairy Princess with Butterfly wings gave her a gift of 'Be Well' paints and was told to use them with her paint brushes. This Princess's friends were the Seeing-Eye Butterflies.

Adaea had complications in her illness on earth and was called to the Spirit World. The White Creativity Fairy Princess visited who gave her "Magic Angel Wings" and made her an Angel Princess. As the Angel Princess she could be in the Spirit World but still was able help those on Earth find their "Inner Prince or Princess". When you see a star in the sky you know she is painting, dancing & shining her special magic for you.

"Dream of painting on the Medicine Wheel"

2017 - Show in London England

Show with Brigid Marlin & Friends sharing visionary art.

have pleasure in presenting

Brigid Marlin and friends

An Exhibition of Imaginative Art painted in Renaissance techniques.

Exhibition Times: Wednesday, 29 November to Friday, 1 December. 11am - 6pm.
Closing Party: Saturday, 2 December, 11am - 2pm.
Above: Della Burford's painting Miracle Below: Brigid Marlin

See the "Love Wind" painting

"2009 - In a dream going up a stairwell with Russian women and invited to go there"

2018 Visionary Art Conference Moscow

Moscow had a Visionary Art Conference which I was thrilled to be part of ..thanks to all those organizing including Oleg Korolev. I had a painting shown and did a remote speech. I was honored that my painting won first prize for Graphic Art in the Visionary category. I was pleased to be part of this as I feel that our capabilities as humans are so incredible And in a time of being so technically saavy, it is important to remember this. We have revelation, dreams, divine imagination. We can co-create with the divine. Visionary art is important for humankind.

Shaman's Eye by Della Burford

See "Make a Inner Dream Mandala"

50th Anniversary Celebration of the Asaba Art School

Congratulations Kazuko Asaba!

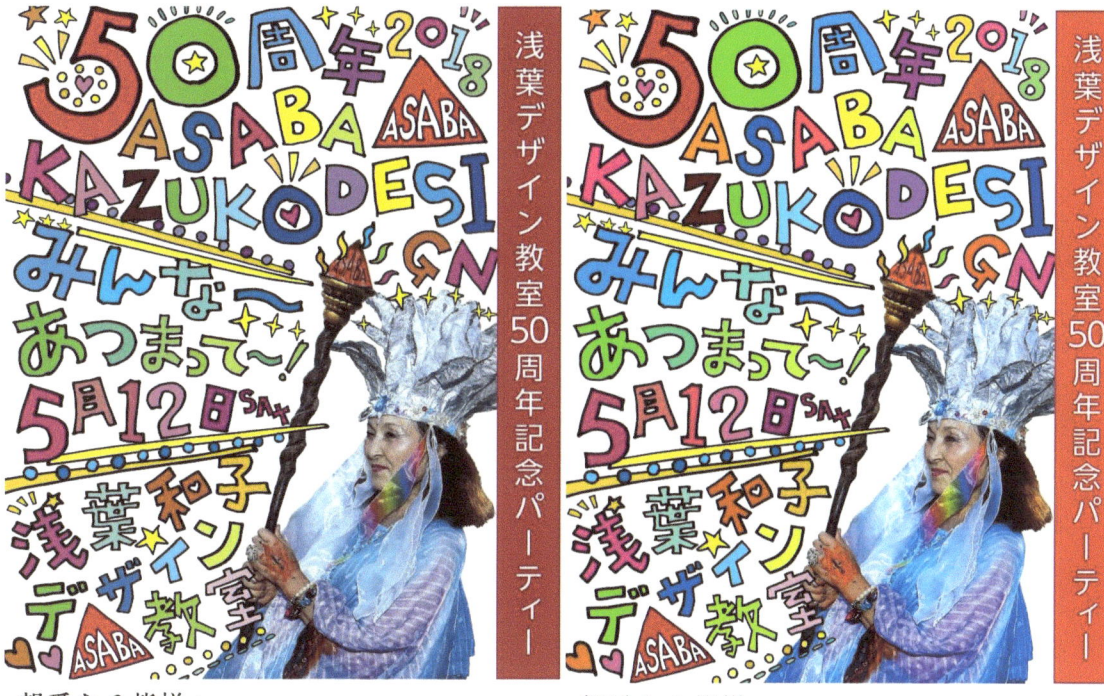

2018 - 50th Anniversary of Kazuko's Art School/Programs

From 1968 to 2018, Kazuko met about 2000 children and had great power and learning from the children.
In 2010, the name of Athabasca Art Square was born that has a design classroom, Art Cafe, and Kanazawa Bunko Art Festival, and has become a place for many people to meet and exchange information. The guests from all over the world are now coming & this included Della and Dale in 2018. Over time, the flowers of life began to bloom. The new departure from the 50th year is she has made a new space, "Warrior of the Rainbow "
for everyone. She hopes to learn the wisdom of her predecessors, and to make sure that they will be able to tell the children of the future. May 16, 2018

Celebrating the 50th Anniversary

Many people came from the community to celebrate the Anniversary of the Asaba Art School. People reached out to say thank you to Kazuko for her great contribution to their children and to the community.

"This is a live dream"
Kanazawabunko Festival Poster

We could hardly believe the colors, life and good energy in this poster. When arriving and going to the Festival we saw the children & performers in their beautiful costumes and the same good energy, colors and life was bursting from eveywhere. We had arrived at a place of our dreams.

"Was asked what is east and west?"
Before going dreamt of dancing children &
adults, rainbow colors and laughter"

2018 - Della & Dale in Japan

We visited Japan. We went to the Kanzawabunko Festival and saw 20 performers and 60 children in my (Della's) story Magical Earth Secrets called in "Majical Rainbow". Kazuko was a fabulous host. We loved seeing her and Ruu*Ruu again. Ruu*Ruu's costumes were awesome and the performance magnificent. The children added so much too. It was truly magical.

"had a dream of a white flower that when I thought a color it changed and transformed."

Performers in "Majical Rainbow"

Star Bird and Performers who play the Four Season are above with myself (Della) and below is Rainbow Wings receiving all of its colors to fly again. Thanks Dale for photos.

Tomomi Shimiza on left with Masa (Winter), Spring, Hiromi Inti Uezmi (Fall), & Uoomin Asami (Summer).

Rainbow Wings receives full colors. Rainbow Wings performed by Momoko Sudo.

"In a dream saw a Parade of costumes and many with magic wands!"
2018 Performers are together!

All the performers are finally together! They look beautiful in all their colors - ready to give a message to love and protect the world.

Ruu*Ruu, front Tomomi Shimiza, Kazuko Asaba with a friend, Yuhki Oomoto, Satoru Ugajin, Ricky Risa Nishzawa, Momoko Suda, and in the back from right to left Yuki Ishio, Masa, Yu Spring, Tazuko Noguchi, Susumu Tamura, Satri Abe, Uoomin Asami and Hiromi Inti Uezmi- missing is Yuko Nawa Inui and Fiori Hanawo the - musician. etc.

"In 2009 saw Kazuko dressed in gold"

Meeting boy who was first "Rainbow Wings" in Japan

Meeting the performer who performs Sweetwater Yuhki Oomoto and her sons. Her son on the right, Kazumi was the first boy in Japan performing Rainbow Wings in 2013 when he was a child.

Della and Kazuko

Della and Yuki Ishio

"had a dream of a Sun Ray family"
2018 - Majical Rainbow live!
"Majical Rainbow" makes the book "Magical Earth Secrets" become alive!

Satoru Ugajin as SunRay

Della and Dan Asaba

Tomomi Shimizu as StarBird

Ricky Risa Nishizawa as Earth Seed

"I was told in a dream to storytell in Japan a story with the world at the center"

Storytelling - Dream Gifts for the Planet Earth

The "Dream Gifts for Planet Earth" is the story about meeting the Eight White Sacred Animals & light beings who give us gifts to keep ourselves in balance & make dreams for the Planet Earth's health.

"Saw ethereal white animals together - all dreaming"
Della Storytelling & Sharing books

I did a storytelling at the Asaba Art Centre and showed paintings from Dream Gifts for Planet Earth. I also shared the book Art for One World - a book about three Magical, Mystical Adventurers & ideas to make a difference.

"Had a dream of a white buffalo dance .. 2014 also in the 1980's had a dream of my mother becoming a white buffalo"

Sharing another Dream story

In the Dream Story I tell of the White Buffalo who appears to remind us to remember our connection to the sky and the peace of ourselves and our planet. This mandala story came from meeting eight sacred white animals in my dreams.

"In my dream I see an giant eye.. in the center the sun .. the world.. a sphere of light"

More Storytelling in Japan

Below more painting to the Land of the Sacred White Animals. Above we journey into the Giant Flower Islands where the flowers are as big as houses in Dodoland.

As synchronicity has it the boy on the left came to the storytelling in a Firebird costume he made - it was like the Phoenicorn walked into the room which is the main character of the journey.

"In my dream I said a line of poetry and the image appeared."
Della painting & meeting many new friends!

I (Della) shared an Ocean painting technique of painting abstract grounds. Dale and my mother Desiree have often painted Öcean"painting with me. My mother taught me about abstract grounds and letting the paint speak.

Della sharing her Öcean"way of painting.

Meeting Naoka Watanabe, an author who shares a love of books & puppets.

"Saw many holy ones meditating in my dreams"

Asaba Art Square Events

Many exciting events happening at the Asaba Art Square. We (Della and Dale) saw the Hawaiian Dancers & Singer. We also visited the Mandala class where they were doing "Yantra" painting with Mr. Dipock, a teacher whose family in Nepal has been doing mandala art since the 14th century.

"Saw buddha in my dream with a jewel"
"Said rainbow & one appeared - silence & stillness"

Great Buddha & Bamboo Garden

There are many powerful and sacred places in Japan. We (Della and Dale) felt fortunate to visit the Great Buddha in Kamakura and the Bamboo Garden with Kazuko and Ruu*Ruu . Many buddhas in my dreams.

The statute of Buddha was at least forty feet high.

This bamboo was about 18 inches across.

"running in a field & the fabric changing colors"
Visiting the La la la Studio.

We went to the La la la Gallery in Tokyo and were asked by Erico Shiomi to be part of a tapestry Peace Project that involves many people internationally. They are making a huge tapestry of fabric pieces created by different individuals in the world from old kimonos that were retreived from a kimono shop after the 20111 earthquake. They also make some of them into stage costumes. They hope it will be the drop curtain of the cultural hall in Ishinomakin in the future.

Erico with a book of costumes from her former teacher Emi Wada who designed costumes for the 7th Samurai.

"Saw many dreams of costumes as has Ruu*Ruu"
Tokyo - Visiting Ruu*Ruu's Studio

We visited Ruu*Ruu studio, and we all saw some new designs for costumes Ruu Ruu is making for my story "Miracle Galaxy" which is the story of the eight healing Angels. Many are Goddess - like and come from dreams.

"I should make a special power necklace"
Beads & Friends in Tokyo

Ruu*Ruu's friend Jasmine showed us around one area of Tokyo. She loved one of Dale's beaded amber necklaces he was showing. We are still "into beads" after all these years since getting our first beads in Morocco in 1971. We felt lucky that Ko, one of Dale's former students, visited us in Japan from Korea.

Ko Jason from Korea visits us in Ruu*Ruu's studio.

"saw an eye with a medicine woman in the center"
2018 - Children's Peace Pipe

The Children's Peace Pipe given to Della Burford 35 years ago was gifted to Kazuko Asaba which is for the children of the world. It is symbolic of the vision we share to wish the best for the children of the world and for world peace. The song of the Children Pipe has the words: "Oh children of the universe, let us live in a place of peace. Where there is love, and where there is light, and where the eagles fly so high." This song was sung in ceremony many times by a medicine one and also used in an introduction of the performance of Magical Earth Secrets in New York, this was before the story was a book and this performance went to all the children in East Harlem.

"In a dream I saw the Dream Goddess who stamped her foot and the earth shook"
Warrior of the Rainbow Space

Kazuko started a new "Warrior of the Rainbow" space in her Asaba Art Centre. There was a storytelling by Kanako Sakaguchi and a rainbow lunch. There was a big Typhoon the day before & the hotel we were in shook for three hours and windows broke. I remembered my dream of the Dream Goddess who said "The earth will shake to remind us of our responsibity to take care of the earth." At her new space Kazuko has created a Rainbow Archway for entering.

"People in a circle all holding a lit candle!"
The Community comes to hear the storytelling!

Stories are alive and well in Japan. We were thrilled to attend this storytelling in Kazuko Asaba's new "Warrior of the Rainbow" space. We feel gratitude.

"I will have beauty in my life.. I am in the place of the hummingbird" When back in Canada saw the Eagle Wand - same as a lucid dream (1973) & then still dreaming - a real eagle and when I said rainbow a circular rainbow circled the eagle. Also a dream of the Earth with a rainbow zooming around it - in the center people on a ferris wheel".

Meeting at the Rainbow Archway

Della "Bird Woman", Kazuko "Peace Creator", Ruu*Ruu – "Cosmic Designer"and Dale – "White Eagle" met at the Rainbow arched gateway. We are sending our good wishes to the children of the world and all those that have and will create Ärt for One World" and their Milestone Books to share with the world. We visualize the world strong and healthy. The world and moon have a circular rainbow around them!

Art Activities to do for Art for One World

40 Art/Writing/Costume Activities

Milestone Book Questions & Part 1 and Part 2   *p203-5*

Story Map for Imaginary Picture Book   *p206*
Travel Adventure Story/Paintings

Inner Dream Mandala   *p207*
Journey to the Giant Flowers

Dream Diary/ Dream Wheel Egyptian Story Mural   *p208*

Create a Healing Story   *p209*
Dancing Body Rainbows or Cushions

Cosmic One   *p210*
Create Your Own Myth

Picture with a Frame
Rainbow Hat   *p211*

Enviro – Hero/Heroine/Helper
Story Map for an Environmental Picture Book   *p212*

Enviro – Hero/Heroine Short but Good Story   *p213*
Illustrations for Environmental Picture Boo

Title Page, Dedication Page and Cover for Picture Book
Enviro-Puppets   *p214*

Color and Sound   *p215*
Magical Earth Costumes/Play

Wind Dance   *p216*
Lovewind Painting

Environment Sets   *p217*
Body Energy Rainbows

Make a Necklace
Four Winds – Four Directions   *p218*

Nature Wish Mural   *p219*
Metamorphosis

Enviro-Earth Song   *p220*
A Wish for the Earth Big Book

Environmental Play   *p221*
Nature Prince or Princess

The World we Love   *p222*
Sensory Journey

Time Mandala   *p 223*
Ocean Painting

Eagle Hat   *p224*

Bird Helmet   *p225*

Answer these questions- for your Milestone Book
Milestone Book Part 1 and Part 2
I have included a few examples with page numbers
from Art for One World as inspiration.

WHO
Who are your tribe? p16, 30, 179, 198, 233, 227-230, 231
Who are your family? p31, p179, 196, p229, p230, 232
Who believes in you? 29, 71, 92, 99, 139, 198, 227-230 231, 232
Who has influenced you? 21, 29, 33- 35, 70, 162, 166-67, 171
Who has inspired you? p3, p 23, p41, p11, p68, p79, p111, p151
Who are your Power Animals/Plants/Flowers? p52, p151, p32
Four Winds/ Four Directions Mandala/Giant Flowers

WHAT
What – What are the Milestone in your life?
(Important events – Art/Celebrations/Rites of Passage)
(Important events from the time you were born till now)
23,33,38,41,46,50,55 66,79,89,92-3,100,108,114,125,128,141-4,178
What is the Culture you come from? p49, p192, p88
What is your Spirit Home? p40, p49, p154-155, p158
What Ancient Culture do you relate to? 27, 33, 40, 49, 79, 96
What is "Good Medicine" for you? 35, 53, 69, 195-196, 135, 171
What are your Dreams for the Future? p139, p153, p178, p199
See the Time Mandala / Egyptian Story Mural
See the World We Love Activity/ Nature Wish Mural

WHERE
Where did you travel first to? p12, p16, p21
Where were travel adventures? 23,27,40,41,44,49,50,60,69,77
78,80-84,96,99,100,102,104,112,121-22,126,128,129,155,162-4,192
Where did you fall in love? p11, p40 (with a country)
Where did art become story- theatre? 36,37,38,48,50,51,54,56,57
59,62,63,71,72,74,76,87,91,93,94,95,97,99,104,109,119,126,128,143
Where did you share your love for another country?
p77, p78, p80, p81, p82, p83, p84, p113, p181, p192
Where did you visit that was sacred? 40,60,100,102,121,135,192
See Travel Adventure Story & Painting
For art/story to theatre see the **When** activities

HOW
How did you have transformation in your live? p13, p22, p 27
How did you change problems to solutions? p15, p45
How did you remember your dreams? 26, 58, 123, 131, 151, 188
How did you find your inner world? p13, p85, p103, p167
How did you become more intuitive? p26, p33-34, p88, p125
How did you make masks? p20, p42, p48, p54, p70, p142
See Inner Dream Mandala
See Dream Diary/Dream Wheels

WHEN
When was wonder in your life? 63, 79, 80, 82, 93, 95, 97, 143
When did you do mandalas? 26, 35, 71, 112, 48, 163-64, 170, 179, 191
When did you share your paintings? p136 -138, p147- 48, p150, p155-56, p158-9, p165, p168, p175, p176, p186-189, 190-194
When did you feel kindness? p 21, p145, p152, p172-175, p193
When did you feel love for nature? p74, p93, p149, p160, p161 p169, p182, p183, p184, p185, p186-189
When did synchronicity happen? p33, p73, p120, p189, p196
See the Environmental Picture Books/Enviro-Puppets
Nature Prince/Princess/ Sensory Journey
See the Magical Earth Costumes/Play - Environmental Play
See Story Map for Imaginary Picture Book
See Ocean Painting/ The World We Love

WHY/WHEN
Why/When did you have a miracle happen? p110, p117, p123
(or know someone that did experience a miracle)
Why/when did you feel a healing (give or receive) in your life?
p15, p16, p40, p46, p57, p59, p62, p91, p105, p106, p122, p124
Why/When - a mystical experience? p33, 39, 40, 103, 123, 127
Why/When did you feel an angel? p64, p105, p106 , p133, p157
When/When did you feel the presence of a Cosmic One?
p36, p40, p43, p61, p98, p130, p132, p146
Why/When did you feel something divine? p16, p37, p40
p86, p31, p132, p140, p146, p191
See Create your own Healing Story
See Cosmic One Art / Create Your Own Myth
Body Energy Rainbows/Dancing Body Rainbow

Milestone Book Part 1
Who, What, Where, How, When and Why

1. Write up a **MILESTONE GRID** with the years of the Milestones – Answer the **WHO** and **WHAT** questions -. **People involved** - family tribe - influencers - Inspirers - Power Allies **Special Events** - could be Sports/Arts/Rites of Passage. It is important to include Feelings or special moments from the Events. What is your **CULTURE** you come from? , What is the Ancient Culture you identify with? What is "**GOOD MEDICINE**"for you?
   See the Four Winds/ Four Directions Mandala

2. On your Milestone Grid include Both **WHAT & WHERE** questions.
   Where did you **TRAVEL**? Where did or do you live? Where did you fall in love?
   Where is your **Spirit Home** where you feel most at home.
   Next describe your life from when you were born up to the **PRESENT**t in your life
   Third - What do you wish for the **FUTURE**
   See the Travel Adventure, Time Mandala Activity

   How were all of these recorded e.g. Diary or photos/art – collect these and put them on the page with the short feeling paragraphs
3. Make a **TRANSFORMATION MAP** and answer the question HOW
   How did you have transformation in your life?, How did you change **problems to solutions?** If you remember you dreams tell how ? How did/do you feel more intuitive or feel the divine. See Create your own Healing Story.
   Dream Dairy/Inner Dream Mandala

Milestone Book 2 - It can be a collaboration

4. Answer the questions **WHEN**
   When was there **WONDER** in your life?, when were you **CREATIVE?**
See the Imaginary Story Map
   When did you feel the Wonder of Nature? When did you feel synchronicity?
   Collect photos of your creations. Collect photos of yourself in nature.
   Express what you love about nature.
See the Environmental Picture Book

5. Answer the question **WHY** in relation to A **MIRACLE or HEALING**
   in your life or someone around you Why or How did you have a Miracle happen?
   Why & How did you feel a Healing? Did you ever feel a mystical experience or an angel?
   Did you ever feel a Cosmic One? Did you ever feel something Divine?
   See Create your own Healing Story and Cosmic One

6. Assemble all parts - .each part can be a separate chaper
   It came to me in a dream that this could be a **collaboration**.. you doing the writing or art and someone else helping with other part. Saw a book in my dream written by one person and the art of another.. in the dream the art was abstract.
7. .. See the **Title page, Dedication and Cover Activity to complete**

Story Map for an Imaginary Picture Book

Instructions: Think of a imaginary character using your creativity. Think of where your imaginary character would live. Make a story map. Tape two or three writing paper sheets together to make one long sheet. Draw an imaginary body of water such as an ocean, lake, pond, stream or river. Think of different mountains and some unusual or imaginary houses. Think of some different trees.

Materials: watercolors, felt markers, pencil crayons, writing paper, tape

Follow up: You can do the "Illustrations for Environmental Picture Book" activity Card but instead make it an imaginary story instead of an environmental story. In writing the story instead of having an environmental problem you can think of a problem that can happen in the society around you .. like for instance loneliness or bullying. Your story will include solving a problem in a creative and peaceful way.

Follow up: You can make a Imaginary Play.. look at the "Environmental Sets" card to get ideas for making sets for your story and "Magical Earth Costumes/Play " to get some ideas on how to do costumes for your story.
Have fun.

Art & Writing Activity

Travel Adventure Story & Painting

After you travel to a fantastic place in our beautiful world write about it and paint a story. Have a beginning, middle and an end to your story. Think of a conflict you can solve in the story .. it can be a big or large problem but solve it in a creative and peaceful way. If you have not traveled, look on the internet or in a magazine and find a place you would like to go to and write an adventure story with this place as a setting.

Materials: Writing paper and art supplies such as felt markers, pencil crayons and paint.

Inner Dream Mandala

Go into your inner world --imagination or dreams. Your Mandala will have four parts or quadrants. Start by making a collage of photos of of your personal life and then a collage of memorable dreams you remember - this you can draw and may even later want to paint. After doing the collage and drawings you can start the Inner Dream Mandala.

If you feel a connection to any one animal or plant (e.g a particular flower or tree) or feel you have a nature guardian you can include it on the first part of the wheel. The second part will be any positive Imaginative characters you have had in your imagination or dreams that you feel shows qualities you admire. The third part will include someone who you felt helped you Heal when you may not have been well and you may think of them as a hero/heroine of healing. This may be in real life or a dream. The fourth part is a Cosmic One who may have come in a dream, in real life or you can imagine them .. see the 'Cosmic One' card for more details. So one part is Connected to Nature, another to a positive Imaginary character and the next one a hero/heroine of Healing and the last a Cosmic One. All together this will be your Inner Dream Mandala

Materials: Art paper --large enough to draw a large circle, divide in four. felt markers, color pencils, oil pastels, tissue paper, paint

Journey to the Giant Flowers

Instructions: In the Dodoland story you go into Flowers that are Giant and you are small. You feel the colors, the essence and hear music. Sometimes it is a doorway to another world.
Choose a flower (from photo or around you) and imagine going into it, smell the perfume, hear the sound around and feel the energy.
Do a piece of art to represent your journey into the Giant Flowers.
If you have a camera try to take some special photos of flowers to have around you to remind you of the beauty of our world.

Materials: art paper, felt markers, oil pastels, paint. If you have a digital camera take some Flower photos.

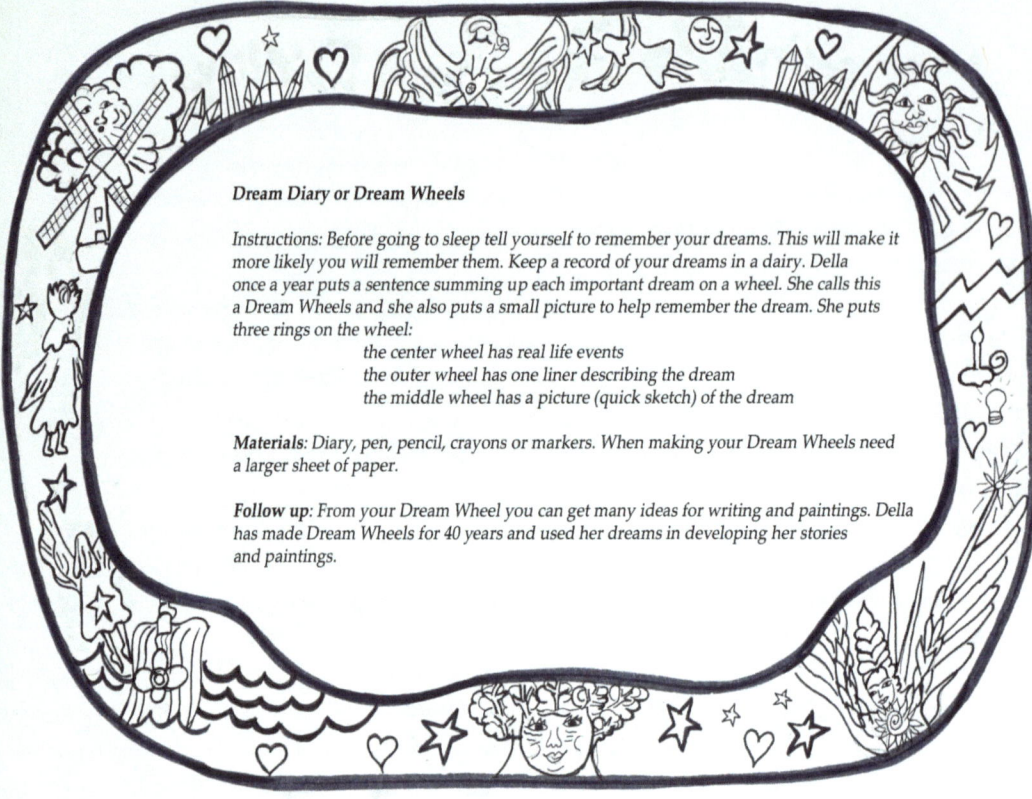

Dream Diary or Dream Wheels

Instructions: Before going to sleep tell yourself to remember your dreams. This will make it more likely you will remember them. Keep a record of your dreams in a dairy. Della once a year puts a sentence summing up each important dream on a wheel. She calls this a Dream Wheels and she also puts a small picture to help remember the dream. She puts three rings on the wheel:
- the center wheel has real life events
- the outer wheel has one liner describing the dream
- the middle wheel has a picture (quick sketch) of the dream

Materials: Diary, pen, pencil, crayons or markers. When making your Dream Wheels need a larger sheet of paper.

Follow up: From your Dream Wheel you can get many ideas for writing and paintings. Della has made Dream Wheels for 40 years and used her dreams in developing her stories and paintings.

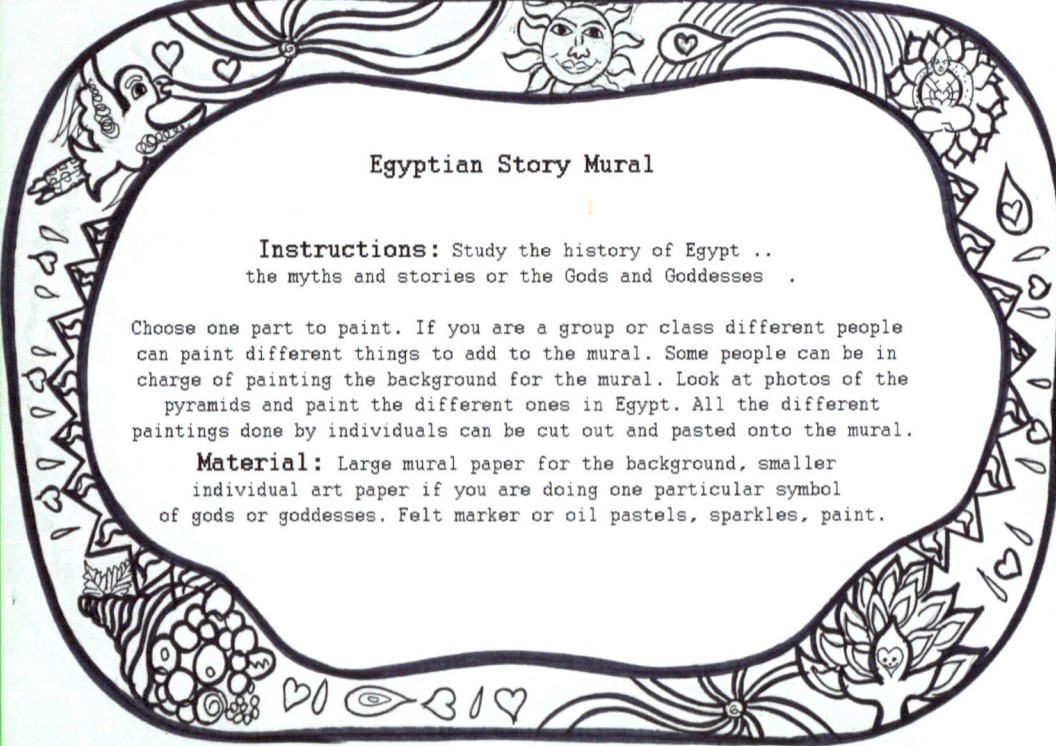

Egyptian Story Mural

Instructions: Study the history of Egypt .. the myths and stories or the Gods and Goddesses .

Choose one part to paint. If you are a group or class different people can paint different things to add to the mural. Some people can be in charge of painting the background for the mural. Look at photos of the pyramids and paint the different ones in Egypt. All the different paintings done by individuals can be cut out and pasted onto the mural.

Material: Large mural paper for the background, smaller individual art paper if you are doing one particular symbol of gods or goddesses. Felt marker or oil pastels, sparkles, paint.

Create your own Healing Story / Angels

Think about sometime in your life when you have not been well and someone that helped you .. write a story about them. As in 'The Create Your Own Myth' activity, do a Story Map and with your story do some drawings or painting. Della has written a story with Seven Angels of Healing from thinking of people in her life who have helped her with the qualities of healing, like good thoughts, peace, having gratitude and kindness.

Material: art paper - felt markers, pencil crayons, paint and art paper

Dancing Body Rainbows or Cushions

Instructions: Do the same activity as the Body Energy Rainbows, lie on a large Piece of white paper and have someone trace around you. But this time instead of standing do a dancing position. Do as you did in the Body Energy Rainbow, draw different things from nature in your body. Do a special bird or animal? Do you see gods or goddesses from other cultures or feel a cosmic one. What colors and patterns are uniquely you. Express your dreams and love for yourself and nature.

Materials: Large mural paper, felt marker or oil pastels, sparkles, paint .. if this is made into a cushion you can use white fabric to do the body rainbow and fabric paint and sew a back on it and stuff it like you would a cushion.

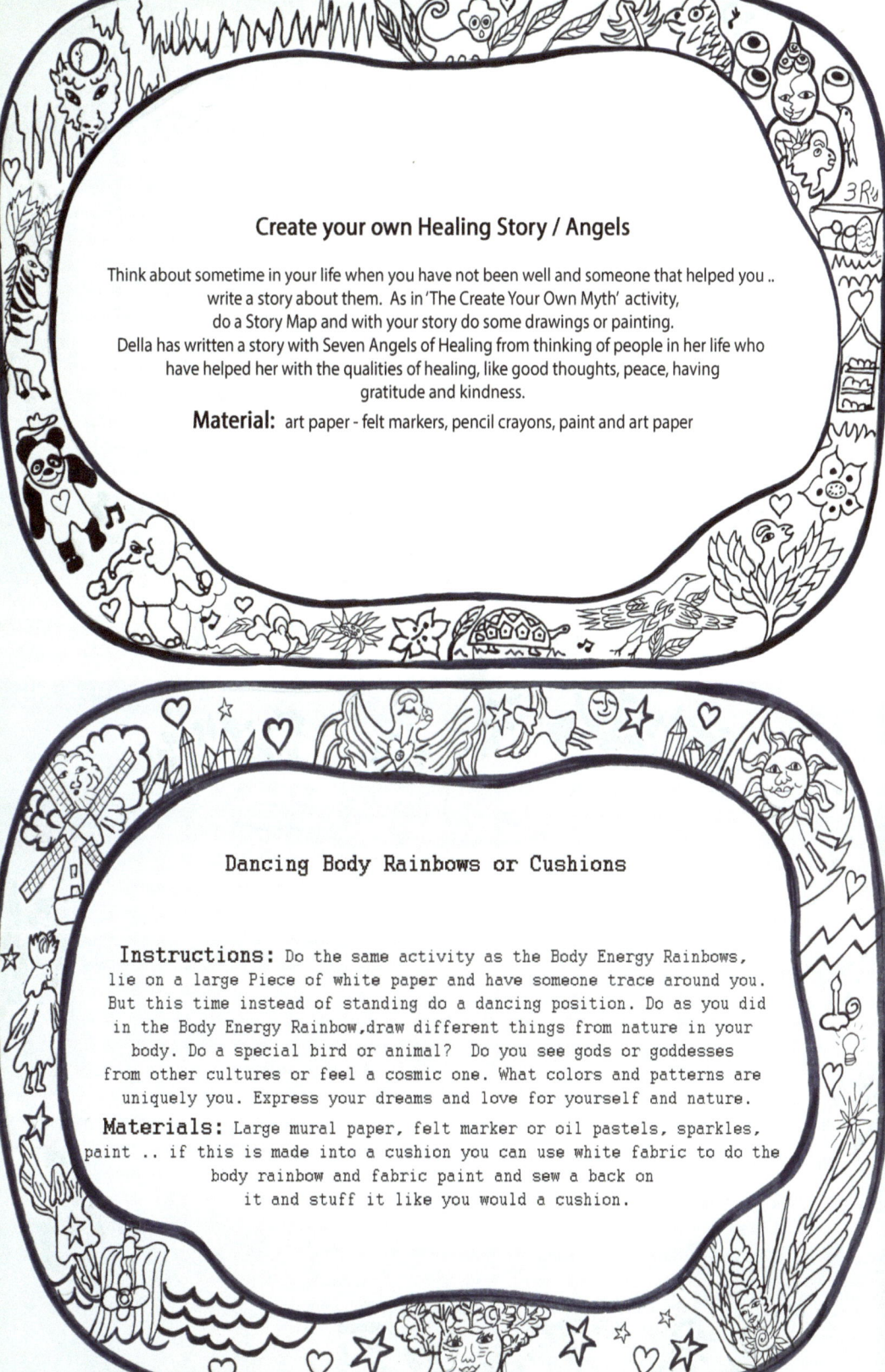

Cosmic One Art

Instructions: When travelling in India, or hearing the myths of Greece or Egypt you hear stories of the Gods and Goddesses and Saintly Ones.
Do a drawing of a Cosmic One, it can be from your own imagination or can be from mythology. Della in her Dodoland story had a Wise One she called 'The Lotus One.'

Materials: Felt markers, pencil crayons, paint or sparkles, art paper

Follow-Up: Your can write a story or even a play including the Cosmic One.

Create your own Myth

Study various myths from around the world. With these as inspiration, write a story using a character you imagine or a character from your dreams. Visualize where this character lives, what its life is like and create a Story Map for it. After doing the Story Map write a mythical story and do the illustrations.

Art Material: writing paper, felt markers, pencil crayons or water colors.
See the Short but Good story activity, Imaginary Story Map and Illustrations Activities

Picture with a Frame

Instructions: Paint a picture of something you love. Cut a cardboard frame for it to help give it a finished look.
Hang them on the wall in a group to have a class exhibition.

Materials: Felt markers or pencil crayons for drawing. Art paper and paint for painting, carboard for the frame.

Rainbow Hat

Instructions: In the story of the Eagle Child Rainbow Wings a rainbow is received as the secrets are learned to love and protect our earth. Draw a rainbow on cardboard (or on paper and glue to cardboard) that is a few inches wider than your head.
Paint it all the colors of the rainbow. Make a band to attach it to with a stapler.
Wear the rainbow and know you are loving and protecting the earth.

Materials: felt marker or oil pastes, sparkles, paint, art paper, cardboard for backing, strip of paper for a band, stapler to attach.

ART ACTIVITY CARD
ENVIRO-HERO/HEROINE/HELPER

Instructions: The eagle child called Rainbow Wings got help from the "little people"- Earth Seed, Sweet Water, Sun Ray, Love Wind, Star Bird and Crystal Wish. Think of what an Environmental Hero/Heroine Helper would look like that could help the planet. Like Rainbow Wings, your Enviro-Helper can be part one thing and part another. He or she could be part tree, fairy or mermaid. You can give your Enviro-Helper a magical object to hold and/or a special magical power. Use your imagination. You may want to create your character before you think of the environmental problem she or he would solve. Or think of the problem first and then create the character. Problems to think of solving may be helping the endangered animals, trees, stopping air or water pollution or preventing ozone depletion.

Materials: Art paper, one or all of water-based felt markers, pencil crayons or water colours.

Follow-up: See Story Map. Enviro-puppets, costumes or Environmental Play.

CREATIVE WRITING/ART ACTIVITY CARD
STORY MAP FOR AN ENVIRONMENTAL PICTURE BOOK

Instructions: Think of a environmental problem you would like to solve. Create your own imaginary Enviro-Hero/Heroine Helper (see Art Activity Card above). Think of where your enviro-helper would live. Share some ideas before you start. Make a story map. Tape two or three typewriter paper sheets together to make one long sheet of paper. Use markers or pencil crayons. Draw on your map real or imaginary trees. Draw in your own real or imaginary body of water -an ocean, lake, pond, stream, or river. Think of some different mountains and some unusual houses and draw them. What kind of house would your Environmental Hero/Heroine live in and what could that person do to solve the problem?

Materials: Typewriter paper and one or all of water based felt marking pens, watercolours or oil pastels.

Follow-up: Make a 3-D sculpture of the setting from found objects or clay.

CREATIVE WRITING ACTIVITY CARD
ENVIRO-HERO/HEROINE SHORT BUT GOOD STORY

Instructions: Look at your art work of your Enviro-hero/heroine/helper and your story map (see cards under these titles). Have them in front of you. Then write a short story. It does not have to be a long story but it should be a good story. Write a story that explains how some environmental problems are solved in a creative way. You may want to include aEnvironmental Villain in your story (see the card under this name). You can write your story for someone your age or for someone younger. Think about what would interest a younger brother, sister or friend. After you have written a good story get an older sister, brother, mom, dad or your teacher to help you edit it. Make sure each word you use is needed to tell your story. Make sure you have used some exciting descriptive words.

Materials: Typewriter-sized paper—recycled if possible—and pencil or pen.

Follow-up: See card below or Environmental Play Card

ART ACTIVITY CARD
ILLUSTRATIONS FOR ENVIRONMENTAL PICTURE BOOK

Instructions: After your Enviro-Hero/Heroine short story is written (see card under this heading) divide your story into eight parts. Circle each part and put a number beside it. Write your story or type it out in good form. Put a couple of spaces between each of the eight parts so they can be cut out easily when it is time to glue them to the pages. Make an illustration for each part using a typewriter size piece of paper for each one. Try different illustration techniques using pencil crayons, water-based felt marker, water colours, oil pastels with a water colour wash over top, or cut and paste for a collage effect. If felt markers are used with a class, you can buy 10 - 15 packages and have the students share them. After finishing the illustrations, paste the writing for each part on or beside them. The back of the previous illustration may be suitable.

Materials: One or all of watercolour, felts, oil pastels, typewriter-sized paper—recycled if possible.

CREATIVE WRITING/ART ACTIVITY CARD
TITLE PAGE, DEDICATION PAGE AND COVER FOR A PICTURE BOOK

Instructions: Make a title and a dedication page for your book. Put the title of the book, the name of the book's author and illustrator on this page. Decorate it with pictures and on it acknowledge someone who has helped you make the book or someone special for whom you have written the story. For the cover make the three sides that open up about one centimetre larger than the writing paper you have used fothe book's pages. The binding edge should not have any extra length. The book's title and the author's (s) and illustrator's (s) names go on the cover. Use a special type of lettering (straight, fancy, balloon etc.). Design a rough draft of the cover on another piece of paper before you start making the actual cover. After completing the lettering, draw a catchy picture that will make people want to pick up your book. It may be the best one in your book, or your favourite character.

Materials: Cover may be cut of bristol board. You may punch holes and tie together with ribbons or use a plastic coil.

ART ACTIVITY CARD
ENVIRO-PUPPETS

Instructions: Draw an imaginary environmental hero/heroine or helper. Remember the helpers in the Magical Earth Secrets book were Earth Seed, Sweet Water, Sun Ray, Love Wind, Star Bird and Crystal Wish. Create your own character. Make it large enough to fill the page. Now you can use this as a pattern for a stick puppet. Put paper on top and trace around the design. Cut this out for your pattern. Lay this pattern on a piece of felt. Always lay your pattern close to the corner so the felt material is not wasted. Trace around the pattern with chalk or crayon so you can see it. Cut out all the pieces. Cut out cardboard for a back. The cardboard must be heavy enough to keep the puppet upright. Glue a flat stick between the fabric and cardboard. Now you have a stick puppet. Work with another person or in a group to make a play. Make a puppet theatre out of a cardboard box.

Materials: Art paper, pencil crayons or water-based felts (for drawing), felt material, glue, sparkles, scissors and a flat stick (for puppet).

MUSIC ACTIVITY CARD
COLOR AND SOUND

Instructions: Sun Ray uses a bow to shoot and give color to the flowers. There are many feelings of color with music. What colors do you feel when you listen to ....classical music....rock music..ethnic music. Without talking. draw the colors and shapes you feel.
Materials: Art paper, one or all of pencil crayons, water based markers, water colours or oil pastels.

DRAMA ACTIVITY CARD
MAGICAL EARTH COSTUMES/PLAY

Instructions: Read the Magical Earth Secret story and think of how you can put on a play or skit. Think of one of the little people in the Magical Earth Story. Do a costume for Earth Seed, Sweet Water, Sun Ray, Love Wind, Star Bird, Crystal Wish and the Eagle Child. Make many costumes. Make masks. Make hats, capes, or wands, Use your imagination. Make eagle child wings to fly. Put on a Magical Earth Secrets play. Have each class do a different chapter of the story. Make an animal dance with Earth Seed, water dance with Sweet Water, fire dance with Sun Ray, wind dance with Love Wind and star dance with Star Bird. Parts of the story can be narrated and songs and dances created.
Materials: Heavy paper (for hats), tissue, foil paper, scissors, felt, found objects or fabric, sparkles, sequins, scissors. If you get white fabric you can paint and add sparkles.
The important thing is to have fun

CREATIVE MOVEMENT ACTIVITY CARD
WIND DANCE

Instructions: Love Wind blows a wind that lets us smell perfume from the flowers. Remember the Love Wind Secret. Feel yourself blowing in the wind. Feel yourself becoming a love wind. Think of someone who needs it and blow them love. Feel yourself a butterfly ...a bird. Feel like the eagle receiving colors. Think of a "Love the Air Dance"

Follow-up: After the Wind Dance you may want to do a "Love Wind Dance" painting.
See photos page 88 and 89.

ART ACTIVITY CARD
LOVE WIND PAINTING

Instructions: Love Wind loves to paint. Mix some tempera colors with lots of water. Drop some paint on the page. It will be runny. Blow the colors around with your breath. Let the colors run into each other.

Materials: paper, tempera paint watered down, brushes. Having containers with one brush per color works well.

Follow-Up: Think of music for your painting or find words that describe things you see in it. Write a poem about your painting.

Art Activity Card
Body Energy Rainbows

Instructions: Lie one a large piece of white paper which is cut to the length of your body and have someone trace around you. Change your shape if you like. The first stage can be done with markers for more detail. Then you can use paint. Think of the elements of nature e.g. sun, air, water or trees. Draw different things from nature in your body. Where in the body would you show the sun, the water, the wind, tree, flower or a rainbow. Do you see a specific animal, or bird? Fill your body with color. Show the energy round your body. What color or pattern is it? Express your dreams and love for yourself and nature.

Materials: Large mural paper. Felt markers or oil pastels, sparkles, paint (one container for each color of the rainbow, and some pastels with colors and white added plus black, white and brown.

Drama Activity Card

Environmental Sets

Instructions: Love Wind loves painting sets. Do a large painting that can be used as a set for your story. See Environmental Picture Book. Use mural paper. Draw the setting and paint it. Draw it large so you can see it at a distance. You may want to sketch it out first before painting. Make it imaginative and colorful. Tape or staple it to create a special mood for your play or a special atmosphere for the classroom

Materials: Mural paper, Tempera paint

Follow up: The set can be used in an Environmental Play.

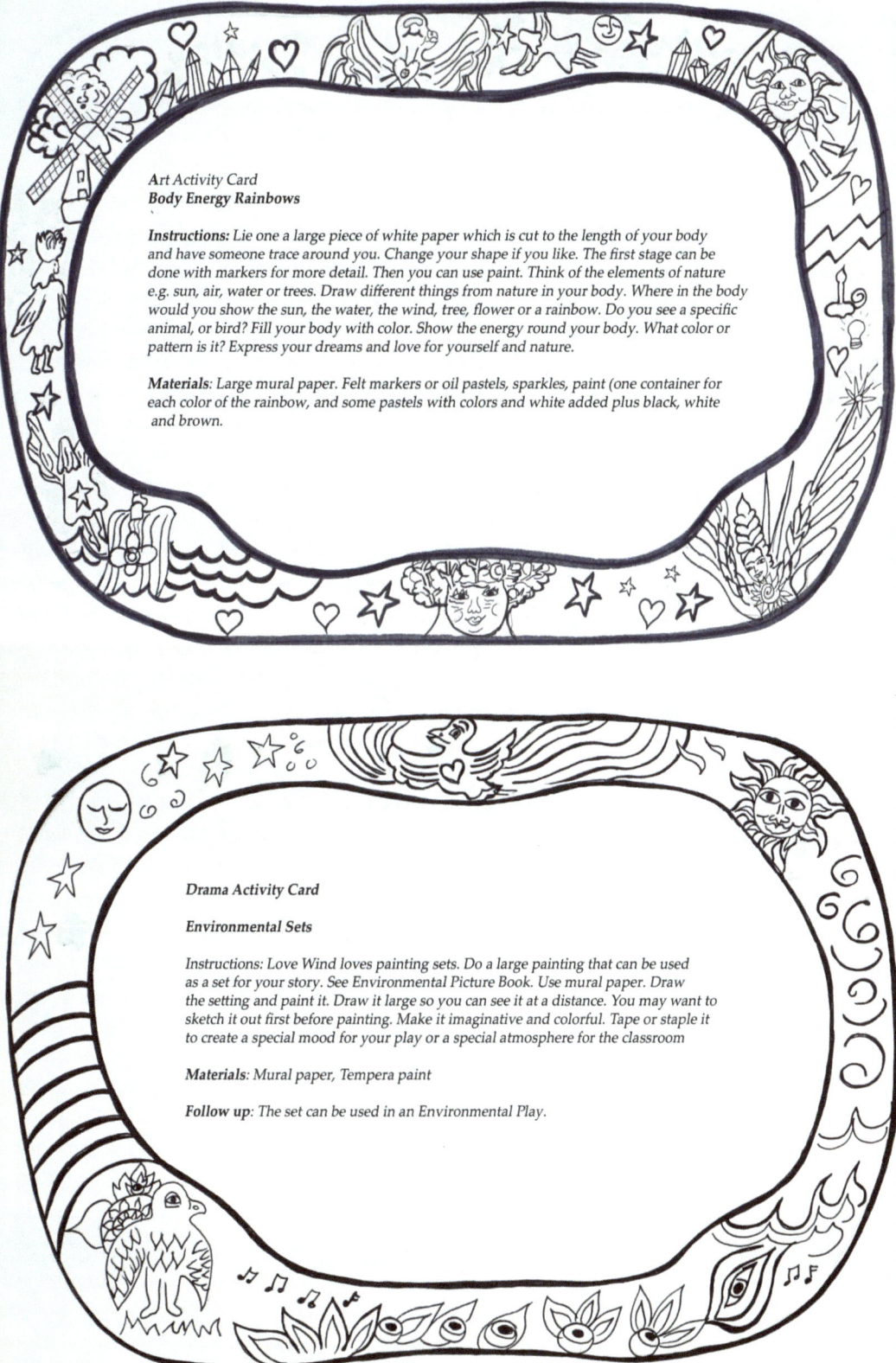

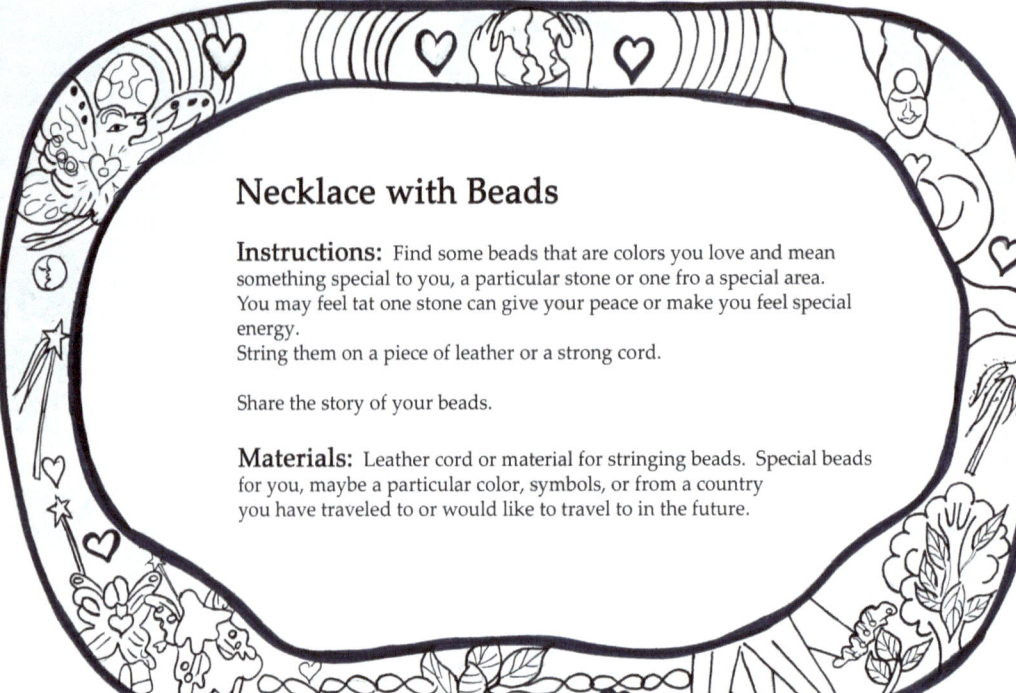

Necklace with Beads

Instructions: Find some beads that are colors you love and mean something special to you, a particular stone or one fro a special area. You may feel tat one stone can give your peace or make you feel special energy.
String them on a piece of leather or a strong cord.

Share the story of your beads.

Materials: Leather cord or material for stringing beads. Special beads for you, maybe a particular color, symbols, or from a country you have traveled to or would like to travel to in the future.

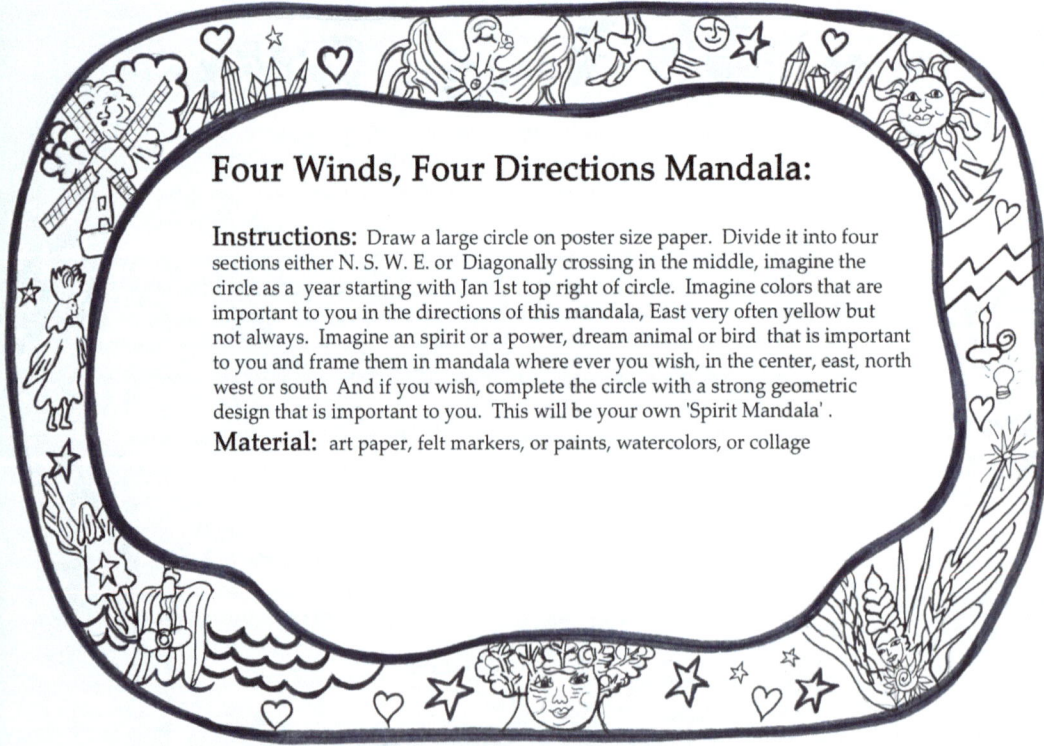

Four Winds, Four Directions Mandala:

Instructions: Draw a large circle on poster size paper. Divide it into four sections either N. S. W. E. or Diagonally crossing in the middle, imagine the circle as a year starting with Jan 1st top right of circle. Imagine colors that are important to you in the directions of this mandala, East very often yellow but not always. Imagine an spirit or a power, dream animal or bird that is important to you and frame them in mandala where ever you wish, in the center, east, north west or south And if you wish, complete the circle with a strong geometric design that is important to you. This will be your own 'Spirit Mandala' .

Material: art paper, felt markers, or paints, watercolors, or collage

ART ACTIVITY CARD
A NATURE WISH MURAL

Instructions: Every person should make a beautiful star - draw, paint or do foil collage. Have everyone think of a wish for "the good of the earth." Put your wish for the earth in the star. Glue them all on a large mural. Paint the background.
Materials: Mural paper, art paper, one or all of a set of water-based felt markers, paint, and materials for a collage.

CREATIVE MOVEMENT ACTIVITY CARD
METAMORPHOSIS

Instructions: Show metamorphosis through movement. Show the transformation of a caterpillar to a butterfly. Show a tadpole growing into an adult frog or an environmental villain growing to be an environmental hero/heroine or helper.

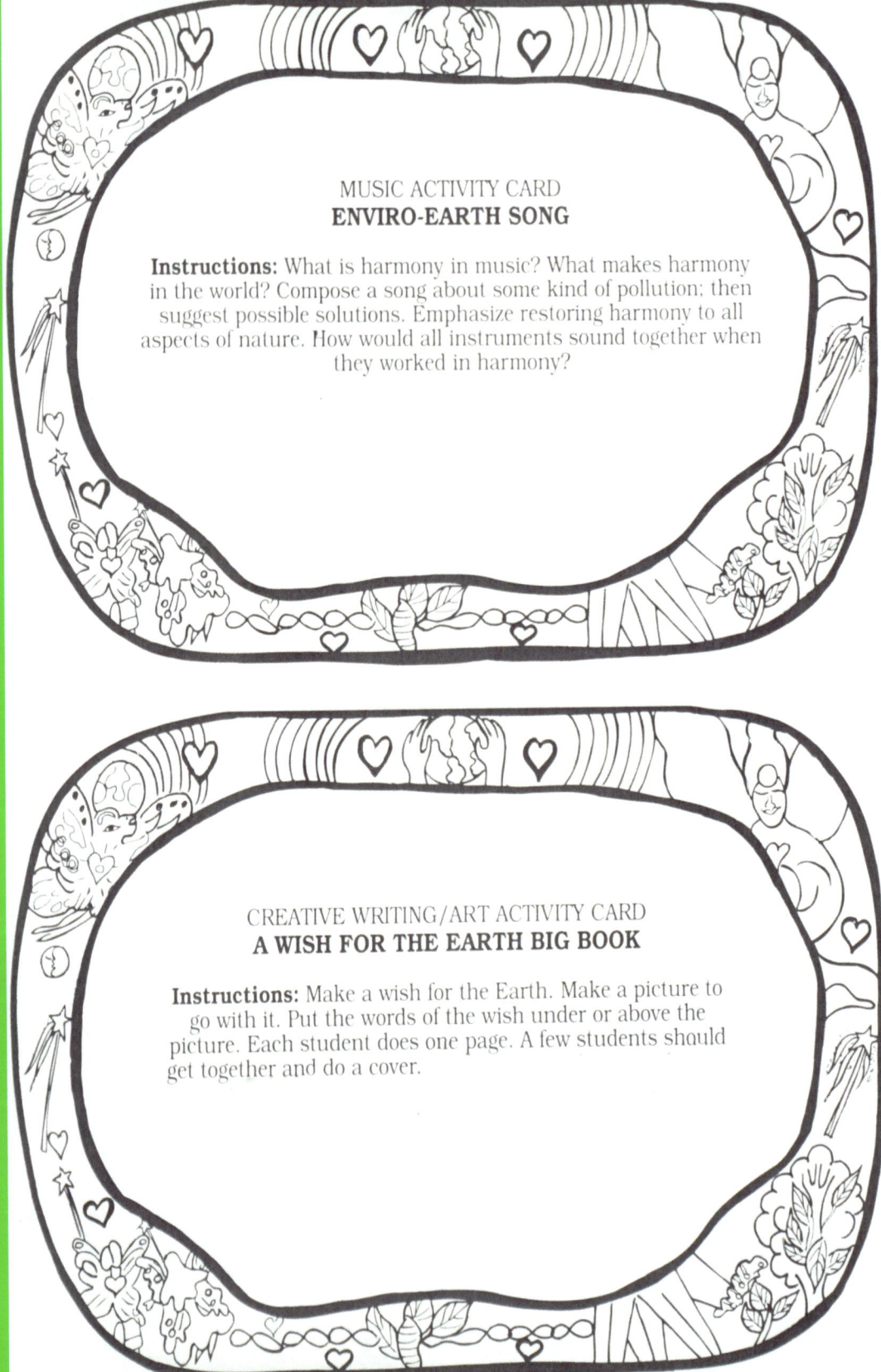

MUSIC ACTIVITY CARD
ENVIRO-EARTH SONG

Instructions: What is harmony in music? What makes harmony in the world? Compose a song about some kind of pollution; then suggest possible solutions. Emphasize restoring harmony to all aspects of nature. How would all instruments sound together when they worked in harmony?

CREATIVE WRITING/ART ACTIVITY CARD
A WISH FOR THE EARTH BIG BOOK

Instructions: Make a wish for the Earth. Make a picture to go with it. Put the words of the wish under or above the picture. Each student does one page. A few students should get together and do a cover.

DRAMA ACTIVITY CARD
ENVIRONMENTAL PLAY

Instructions: Show how an environmental villain transforms its habits and thinking in a story. You may make a play of your environmental story you wrote for your picture book. If you start from scratch, consider conflict and resolution. You may want to look at the Drama Activity Card on Environmental Sets
Environmental Hero/Heroine Costumes
Through the telling of the story or the presenting of the play leave your audience empowered - feeling that they can do something good.

CREATIVE WRITING/ART ACTIVITY CARD
NATURE PRINCE OR PRINCESS

Instructions: Pretend you are a prince or princess, not necessarily because you are royalty but because of your love for all of nature. What would you draw and write? Draw a picture of yourself as a nature-prince or nature-princess and write about your feelings and what you would do to help the Earth.

Materials: Writing paper, art paper, one or all of a set of water-based felts, pencil crayon, oil pastels or water colours.

CREATIVE WRITING/ART ACTIVITY CARD
THE WORLD WE LOVE

Instructions: When Rainbow Wings flew into space and saw the whole world, this eagle child exclaimed "This is the most magical and beautiful thing I have ever seen". Draw a picture of the whole Earth. Write words around the picture of the Earth saying what you love about it. Write from your heart.

Materials: Art paper, a set of water-based markers and/or pencil crayons.

DRAMA ACTIVITY CARD
SENSORY JOURNEY

Instructions: Think of the different chapters of the story of the Eagle Child and take someone on a sensory journey. One group may focus on animals and trees, another on water, air, sun and so on. Each group will think of what they can do to get the feeling of the element they have been assigned without using the sense of sight. They will take someone into their group blindfolded and make them feel the element. For example, for water, a group could have the blindfolded person hear the sound of waves, feel the sprinkle of water on their skin, taste good water, hear the sounds of dolphins, smell seaweed, feel sea shells and listen to the sound in a shell.

Materials: Found objects from home. Be imaginative.

Time Mandala

Instructions: The Mandalas can be worked on as a group or individual. Think of three different times. One is a long, long time ago when life on the earth first started … or going back to an ancient time in history. Second is your life and different things that happened to you since you were born and up to today. Third is the future and how you see your life being. You can put all three times on your individual Mandala or choose one to contribute to a group Mandala.

Materials: *Art paper, large art paper if a group Mandala, felt markers, paints. This can also be done on fabric with fabric paint.*

Ocean Painting

Instructions: *Take art paper and tape to a hard surface like a table. This is so the art piece will dry flat. With a brush put water on the page. You may even pour some water to make puddles. Take ink or paint that is watered down and drop on the page. Let the water make it flow. As you add other colors by dropping you can see how the colors mix. With this kind of painting you have to know when to stop and say it is finished. As it dries sometime you get a surprise. These abstract grounds can by enjoyed by themselves or afterwards you can add a character like an imaginary animal/person on the art. Have fun.*

Materials: *Art paper, masking tape, water, watered down paints or ink.*

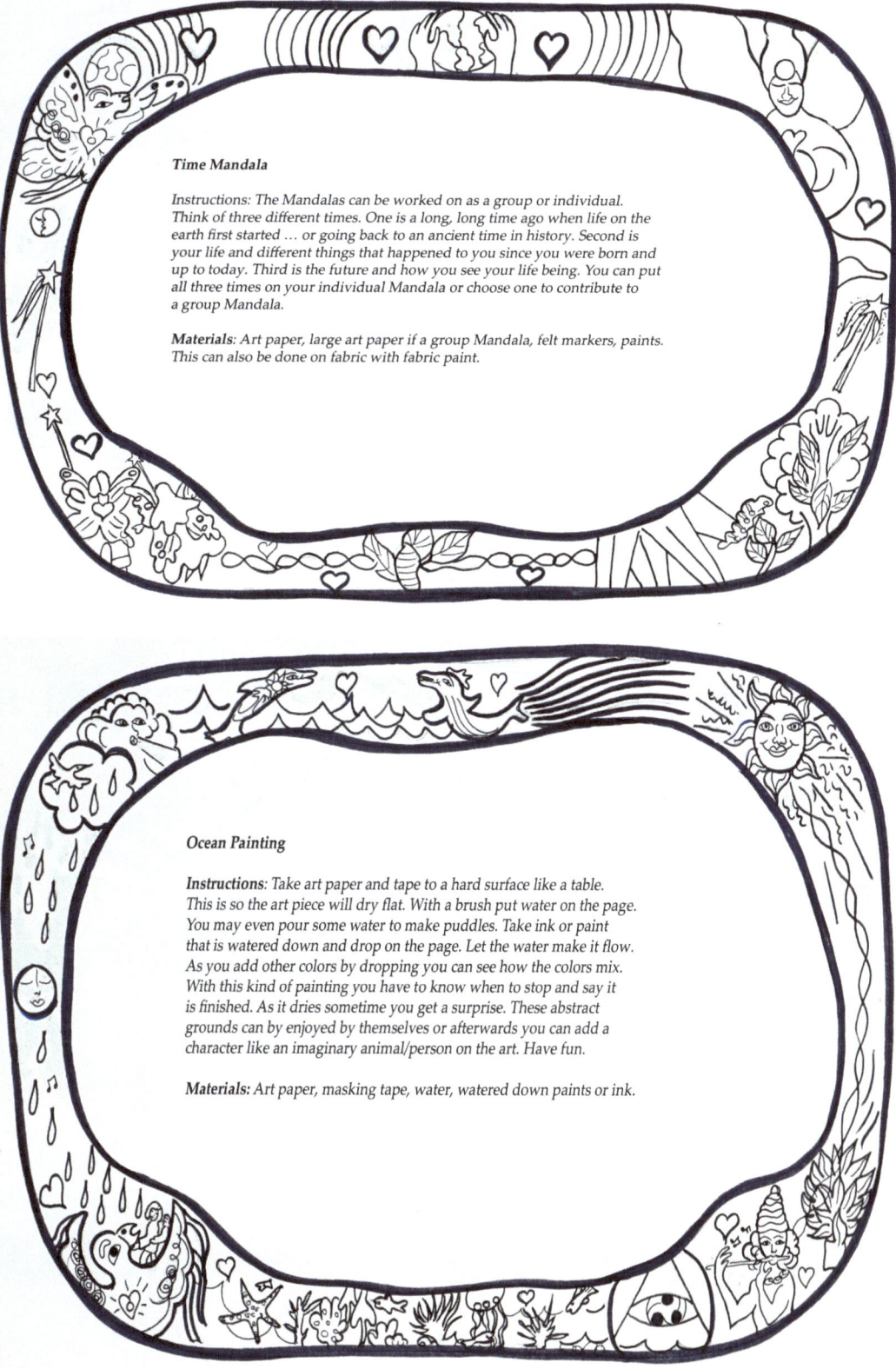

Eagle and Bird Helmet

For both the Eagle and Bird Helmet enlarge to regular paper size. Color all the colors you love. Cut out the bird and staple onto a band. To determine the band put around the head. Hold tight to it as you take it off the head. The hat can be glued onto a construction paper to make it more durable.

Wear you eagle hat to be like Eagle Child and do things for the environment.

Wear the Bird Helmet when you want to be creative and use your imagination

Wear them when doing Art for One World.

Keep it in a special place.

Fly like the eagle!

Cloud Band

Thank You so much!

Our life has been full of support from family and friends, and we want to thank you all! All of the Burford family have been so supportive, like my late mum and dad, Desiree and Lyle. Dales' mum Mary, for helping us in so many ways. My sister Norah, for helping organize our Bali events and so much more. Chris for helping us with the Dodoland website. We enjoyed being in Bali with his family Elissa and Dane. Glen, for this technical advice and both him and Brenda for always being there for us. Thanks to Laura, Ben. Calum & Emma and Rob too, who helped us in building our house. Warren, for his musical energy and sharing being in Bali with us & Tempi & David. Donna, who is assisting from spirit world, and her daughters, Holly and Flora, who we always enjoy seeing. Murray, who we enjoyed traveling to India with & his family Golda and Ewan, and also the joy of O.V.'s Myriam and Elle & families. We are thankful to cousins who live in Naniamo, Jack, Lucy and Sharon and also our cousins living in other locations. Some came to Bali - Stella Beniuk, Karina & family. Our "other" family the Williams, who are always there for us and we thank them so much, too. Tom and Joanne (Sal), with whom we have enjoyed countless moments of fun, Barney, who is one of the original Dodolanders, & Buffy and their family. Rainbow, Sarah who have been an inspiration, and their family. Ollie, who has always been there. Liberty, Arron, & their family. I have included The Princess story in the Divine Section for their daughter Adaea.

Many friends, when Dodoland was created in the Beginning Cycle (1968 -1974), became fantasy animals on the Dragon Ship. We want to thank Tom and Sal (Baby Panda and Seeing Eye Butterfly), George Boddington (Brigadier Smutley), Bruce McCarthy (Wonder Walrus) & (Wise Owl), Bob Richardson (Freddy the Frog), Virgil Scott (Half Past Seven), who is constantly amazing us with his music, Shirley (Lady Smutley), who hosted Dodoland at her school, Loosie Parres (Brenda (Oh La La the Giraffe), who has been one amazing playmate, & Terry Brown, (Dancing Bear) John Mcleod, Ava (Dancing Flamingo), Jeannie Thomas (Flutter Flump-like), Michael Wesslink (Banana) & Russell Coull, Thanks also to friends - Tom and David Walsh. David hosted me coming to Toronto for the Make an Angel. Other lifelong friends we made at this time are Doug and Jules Atkins, Mary Lyenn Ogilvie, Edna Reti, and Pat and Jim Peircey. I think of and thank Aroon and Indur Shivdasani, who gave us a base in India to travel from and have kept in communication over many years

In our second Cycle of Birth (Transformation (1975-81)), I thank the kind people at 3HO in Toronto who taught Kundalini Yoga. Big thanks to Doug Riseborough for the introduction to Dr. Dick Mazurek who published Dodoland and Paul Showalter who did the design of the book. Also want to thank Elisa Lodge, who was friends with me at the time, and later introduced me to Tedrian Chizik who took Dodoland & made it a improv play that toured New York for seven years. Still friends today to some of the people who were in the production – Merian Soto, who was the Flamingo, Jerry Shrair and Julie Lyonn Lieberman who both helped with music. I want to thank all the people doing Production and the places where we were able to share the story of Dodoland. Also Deborah Rothrock, Larry Karush, Desiree Vasquez, Pepon, Raphael Fernades & Larry Stochol. Thanks to my friend Pat Brennan, who came to New York with me when picking up the Magical Earth Secrets costumes. Thanks to Eli and Lala Paper who as children we knew then and still see them in Toronto. Thanks to Harri Maki, Mitchell Gold. Mairlyn Belec, Roman Bittman, & Paul Hugh Khan Skyrider.

In our third cycle of Medicine (1981-87), I want to thank the strong medicine given by all the people who were part of the Production of Dodoland in New York and also the Production of Magical Earth Secrets in East Harlem. I also want to thank Howard Jerome and Alice Brownlee who helped in many ways such as script writing and Alice doing sign language. Also Tree for her costume ideas and Michael Golland for sharing time with us in Mexico. Also David Melville who arranged for me to work with his inner city kids. I think of Deborah Dunleavy, Noami Tyrell and her mother Lynne, Michale Jordana, & Bev Couse. I also want to thank Nicholas Roerich, whose painting were an inspiration to me at this time. During this time we thanks Dr. Binder for this guidance.
We say meegweeth to Vern Harper, and Pauline Shirt who I would like to thank for their balancing energy and letting us share our work with the children at Wandering Spirit. Norah and I lived in a tipi where I wrote Magical Earth Secrets and thanks for her energy. I want to thank the many people in the Kootenays energy who were part of the creation. I also want to thank Kajsa Dolstom, from Globetree in Sweden, who organized the Future Conference - here I met Made Sijia and Made Sidia and later his family who have become lifetime friends. I also have to thank the Inner City Angels for arranging for us to do so much work in the schools. Karin Clifford, Brenda Parres, and Jane Howard Baker. This was invaluable for me to develop the work further. Dale wants to thank Bill Meilen who shared so many connections in Wales for his "Merlin" Quest. He also wants to thank the late Dr. David Davies who believed in his work and made an introduction to

to Everild Helweg Larson Young. Dr. Jordan Paper also toured Wales with Dale. Leo Del Pasqua is to be thanked for this beautiful illuminations from the writings. Dale also wants to thank Mark Jenkins for apprenticeship. He also wants to thank Bill Hawkes for sharing the love of antiques. They worked together at the Harbourfront Antique Market for seven years. We thank Marilyn Belec & Roman Bittman for sharing times together. In the anitque realm in Vancouver Dale thanks Dr. Bill Cameron, Harley Glesby, Evan Elkin, & Jim Roberts. Also want to thank the collectors Bruce Whitehourse & Patti Whitehouse who purchased my Third Eye painting.

In the fourth Cycle of Wonder (from 1989 1995)- this Cycle Magical Earth Secrets was published and I have Paul George, Adrian Carr and Sue Fox and the Western Canada Wilderness Committe to thank. Thanks also to Tom and Eileen Lyons & Dr David Suzuki for their global concerns. Dr. David Lertzman for storytelling collaboration. Dorothy Washburn I thank for her openness to doing Dream work at Christie school. Peter Duryea for his Tipi Camp. I want to thank The Artist in Community Program that I graduated from at Queens University and insight to allow me to do my practicum in a Production of the Magical Earth Secrets by Maria Formolo at the library in Edmonton. Thanks to so many people who were part of this – Maria, Noreen Crone Findlay, and Pauline LeBel. Thanks to many teachers who worked with me on programs: Ann Donald, Jim Rule, Eileen Radiemaker, Ann Breslin, Mary Anne Dente, Bob Davidson, Anna Hall, Helen Ducharme, Pat Flood, Mary Sanders, Mary Pudelsky, Sue Cousland, Kathie Baker, Lilian Clinton, Mary Scambara, Madame Spears and Maxine Goldberg, in Toronto and Sue Ashworth for the Writer in Residence programs in Edmonton. Thanks to the Friends of the Environment Foundation. And a big thanks for the Canada Council Reading Program and Writer Union.

In the fifth Cycle of Third Eye (1996 -2002) Dale and I worked in Mexico and I want to thank so many students, and people at the school.Particularly other teachers, like Grace who arranged for us to be there, Francis Seaton, Laurie McHale, Wallace Murray, Sharlene Ladds, Janice Klassen, Alex, Joy, Ralph to name just a few. We also want to thank Gloria Arroyo, Oswaldo & Oswaldo Jr and Alejandra. A few adventurers in Mexico, Alex, Rick and Renee Watson. On our next adventure we met people in England when we re working there, and Dale was researching Celtic manuscripts. We particularly think of Marian Hall and Elwyn Roberts. We want to thank Penn Kemp, Lynne Moorhouse in 'Sounding of Stones' in Victoria. I have many Doctors to thank as a survivor cancer particularly Dr. Rogers , Dr. Janice Wright, Dr. Teresa Clark & Carol Thatcher working at Inspire Health. Also Dr. Sanders, Dr. Baff, Dale and my mum and dad, and sister Donna who were my main support team.

In the Sixth Cycle of Miracle (2003-2009) I was writing and painting Miracle Galaxy. My sister Donna, was living with us, and helped me. So many people at Inspire Health gave support. We traveled to England to various Sacred Sites and want to thank again, Marian Hall and Elwyn Roberts in England. Thank to Barbera Tremain, and the late Sue Bladdon, who helped arange for us to see the Stone Circles in Cornwall. We visited Mexico and thanks to the village Los Ayala. Worked in Korea and met a woman who became one of my best friends, Jacquie Howardson and have enjoyed time with her and her husband Arnie. We later met Ko Chi Sung & Jang Woo Wang & family who visited us in Canada. I was also fortunate to meet Arron Zerah, & do paintings - Spirit Stories.

In the Seventh Divine Cycle (2010-present), we had 'Spirit of Writing & Art' in Bali. We have Karja to thank for the great studio & collaboration on my Painting Shows. Norah helped me coordinate the event. Many wonderful friends participated and we want to thank everyone. The first held at Balipurnati, we thank Philip Rubinov Jacobsen, Mantra, Vesna, Peter Gric, Irene Vincent, Sylke Gande and Michelle Pettit, Wallace, Susan Melville, Fabrizio Bellardarti, Saharnaz Fara , Grace Po, Francis Seaton, Melissa Matineau, Leema Graham, Eric Bobrow, Ayden Charlyne Chiasson, & Sterling. We are thankful to I Made Sidia, Wayan Suastini, Sugi Sidiaria, & Arix Quric. I went to San Franciso, and was so glad to see my friend Dr. Stevanne Auerbach there. We had a show of the artists from the 'Society for Art of Imagination' in Bali in 2016, and I want to thank all the artists and the organizers, Brigid Marlin & France Garrido, (I have a page with a poster showing the artists). I also showed in Ottawa with the group and want to thank Bhat Boy and in Montreal, the organizer - Jean Pronovost. Later there was a show in New York, and want to thank Brigid Marlin, Olga Spiegel, Miguel Tio, and all the artists I met. Enjoyed lunch - Benny Anderson & family. I was fortunate to be in a show in Moscow and want to thank Oleg Korolev. On Joan Hangarter radio show I talked about Angels, and I felt I had met a kindred soul. We wrote the book with Ian Wallace on Richard Pochinko, and thought of him a lot. Also Robert Moss taught many Dream courses, in which I say thanks. I nurtured many friends interested in dreams. Today, I still chat with Raimonda, Meredith, Darlene, Patti, Alayna, Jen, Caroline, Nan, Shalanhia, Lawrence, Mary Beth, Flo, Wilson, Holly, Margit, Ingrid, Becky, and Cheryl etc. Thanks Yasmin for visiting. People in our house. former Chris, Nate, now- Kelsey, Dan, Joseph & David. Thankful to the people in Japan who have made the book of Magical Earth Secrets into a play - Kazuko Asaba and the costume designer/Producer, Ruu*Ruu. Have included some names on the photos. We loved travelling to Japan in September 2018.
Thanks to Laurien Towers who helped me in this huge edit. Jacquie Howardson for the 2 liner edit, and Nick for the Japanese translation. There are so many people to thank and we are in our hearts grateful. Please forgive us if we have forgotten someone.

All is one, we send our love, Della (& Dale)

Thanks to our family!

Freeman, Brenda, Calum , Emma, Laura, Paul, Glen, Ben Michael, Emma, Dale and myself.. Missing is Rob, Murray, Golda, Ewan, Norah, O.V., Chris, Elissa, Dane, Tempest & David, Emma, Holly, Flora and Lisa.

from R to L Rainbow, Ollie May, Buffy,Tate, Sal -Jo, Kayla, Lauren, Barney,Tavin, Tom, Zayden, Sarah, Ollie, Arron, Liberty & Adaea. Alden to come. Older but my favorite photo.

More Family

My twin Donna - (collective dreaming)

Desiree Burford & Mary Bertrand

Twin Donna & Holly

Rob Burford

Neice Flora

Norah, Chris & Della

Brother Glen & Mum

Thanks so much for helping us travel to Japan and complete "Art for one World".

Love Della and Dale

Top left side: Eli Paper, Myriam Elisabeth Devlin & family, Irene Vince, Chris Martin & family, Norah Burford, Stevanne Auerbach, Janice Klassen, Mary Lynne Ogilvie, Yasmin Glanville, Rainbow Williams & family, Jeannie Thomas. Top right: David Walsh, Gayle Conn Garrison, Tom & Sal Williams, Mitchell Gold, Stella Beniuk & family, Ko Jason, Evan Elkin (not in photo) Also huge thanks to Laurien Tower for editing, Jacquie Howardson for editing two liners,& intro & Nick Muhrin for translating into Japanese and of course Kazuko & Ruu*Ruu

Thanks you's from Kazuko Asaba

Specific thank yous for the book:
1. Della Burford and Dale Bertrand who helped me realize the dream.
2. Aya Kumagai..She gave me lots of advise all the time.
3. Takeshi Ijima .. He also helped in many ways .. for the book -the photos & to make my slides digital.
4. Dan Asaba ... He helped me in so many ways like for finding the many old photos & films.
5. Haru Ijima .. always helping in so many ways
6. RuuRuu... she gave me beautiful costumes and spirit
7. Thanks to Erva Farnsworth for her kindness
8. Thanks to so many for inspiration… to name a few- Keinosuke Sato, Ruth Asawa, Hamza El Deen , Dennis Banks
9. For collaboration on peace projects... Yoshiko Chuma
10. Naoka Watanabe ... She always give me love & humility.
11. Nick Muhrin .. for translating the book to Japanese

General… thank yous:
The children who have attended the school!
The community who has supported events & the café!
Those who made the café meal days!
Those making the Kanazawabunko Festival a success!
Those who have arranged and those participating in international Mandala and Art workshops!
Those that have helped me when traveling!
Those that have arranged and been part of student exchanges! Please forgive me if I have forgotten someone .. so many people have helped in so many ways! Love to all!

"had a dream of a dress for Kazuko - rainbow down shoulders & rainbow down the front"

Celebrating the 50th Anniversary with Kazuko!

Many give thanks in Japan to Kazuko for opening the creative buds in so many children and sharing diversity thru the arts with the community by offering art classes, a community event space and spearheading the Kanazawabunko Festival. We send our love from Canada too! We think of her as part of our family here in Canada. Let's celebrate her, the school, dreams and any art & books that will be created with Art for the One World as inspiration!

Contributors

Della Burford, creator of seven books, leads workshops internationally. She is also a painter, storyteller, & dream adventurer. Della is a former college teacher. After Dodoland was published she devoted herself to painting, writing workshops & books.

Dale Bertrand, author of Druidical Quest & producer of 6 Celtic books has helped create the Environmental Activity Guide.
Dale with a mystical experience has been devoted to sharing Celtic wisdom on his Merlin quest.
He has travelled many countries in the world photogaphing beauty.

Kazuko Asaba is celebrating 50 years of success of her Art School – she also has Asaba Art Centre in Japan which hosts many events. She has helped organize the Kazanawa-bunko Festival which is celebrating its 20th year. She travels the world doing art with children & cultural exchanges.

Ruu*Ruu, a fashion designer, spearheaded 100% Parade & produced "Majical Rainbow" since 2012 in Japan. She had a Hat store in 1988 & designed for various Rock Stars. She met Kazuko in 2011 and they collaborated in getting the story of 'Magical Earth Secrets" called "Majical Rainbow" to the people in Japan.

www.ingramcontent.com/pod-product-compliance
Lightning Source LLC
Chambersburg PA
CBHW040902020526
44114CB00037B/30